MARKET BAR-B-QUE

CONFIDENTIAL

MARKET BAR-B-QUE

CONFIDENTIAL

Michael A. Swirnoff

NODIN PRESS

Design: John Toren

Historic photos are from the private collection of Steve Polski. Additional location photos by John Toren

ISBN: 978-1-935666-86-8

Library of Congress Control Number: 2015955927

Nodin Press
5114 Cedar Lake Road
Minneapolis, MN 55416

*For Sandy, my wife, partner, and best friend,
who has always provided me with support and
encouragement for all of my work;
for Wendy and David, my children, who, no
matter how hard I try, still write better than
their old man; and
for Annie Rose, my twelve-year-old
granddaughter and already a budding writer*

Contents

Little Willard Polski with his grandfather (seated); his father, Hyman, on the left behind him, and two unidentified men who may be Hyman's brothers-in-law, Anthony and Abraham Fineberg.

Introduction

Even since it opened its doors in 1946 at 130 North Seventh Street, the Market Barbecue has been home to celebrities, sport stars, and anyone looking for a great late night meal. (Among family-owned restaurants in Minneapolis, only Jax Cafe in northeast Minneapolis and Murray's Steakhouse downtown can claim a local history that long[1].) Not only did the "Market" fill the stomachs of its rib-hungry customers, it satisfied other appetites as well. Serving as a front for the card playing and gambling obsessions of Willard and Sam, the brothers Polski. A second location in Minnetonka, a western suburb of Minneapolis, lasted for twenty-five years, closing in 2010. Today, the exclusive location is at 1414 Nicollet Avenue on the south end of downtown. The current owner is Willard's son, Steve Polski, and it's operated by Steve's son Anthony.

One of the major reasons for the restaurant's success is the loyalty of its customer base. Today, the Market continues to serve the grandchildren and great grandchildren of the customers who dined at the Market in its early years. As the restaurant moved from one location to another, those same customers and their descendants have continued to eat their ribs at the Market. It has always been the restaurant, not the location, that has attracted these loyal patrons.

---

[1] Probably the longest running restaurants in Minneapolis are Pracna on Main and the Monte Carlo. However, the ownership of these restaurants has changed several times over their long history.

The walls of the restaurant are lined with photos of celebrities who have dined over the years on the Market's pit-smoked ribs and chicken. The Market's website offers this description:

For more than 60 years, Market Bar-B-Que has been serving real pit smoked ribs. Back in the days of vaudeville, Market Bar-B-Que was famous for being the late night spot with great barbeque food. In no time at all, it became the Sardis of Minneapolis, an after hours haven for hungry show folks, sports personalities, and just about anybody who was anybody. That was all back in the days when the Farmers' Market, our namesake, was located across the street. Vaudeville is gone, of course, and things have changed a lot over the years. But we still smoke our ribs just like we used to. And we still get all of the important people stopping in to enjoy our food.

The popular rib joint was the culmination of Sam and Willard Polski's long journey up the "crooked ladder"[2] from early poverty to affluence and respectability achieved by working in a gambling empire in Minneapolis run by another set of local brothers—Davie and Chickie Berman. This tale is about Sam and Willard, and also about their father, Hyman, and his journey from Russia-Poland to St. Paul, Minnesota, where he, too, opened a restaurant—but not before making a layover at the federal penitentiary in Leavenworth, Kansas.

In a recent article in the *New Yorker*, Malcolm Gladwell describes the difficulty experienced by Europeans who immigrated to the United States during the late nineteenth and early twentieth centuries. Many were escaping poverty, pogroms, or conscription into unfriendly armies. Whether Irish, Italian, or Jewish, they were looking for a

---

[2] The term "crooked ladder" was coined by the sociologist James O'Kane to describe how members of ethnic minorities have used organized crime as a vehicle of upward mobility. (O'Kane, James M. 1992. *The Crooked Ladder: Gangsters, Ethnicity, and the American Dream*. Transaction Publishers.) Gladwell's article, "The Crooked Ladder," appeared in the *New Yorker*, August 11, 2014.

better life in America, and many of them found it. But though it may have been a better life, it certainly wasn't an easier life. Making a living was extremely difficult—in fact, income and wealth inequality in the United States was every bit as severe then as it is today.

The passage of the Eighteenth Amendment prohibiting the sale of alcohol presented new opportunities to recent immigrants. A market for booze suddenly opened up to those willing to skirt the law, and offshoots such as prostitution and gambling also provided income opportunities. It wasn't so much that these immigrants wanted to engage in crime; they were simply looking for a path to respectability. That path required money, but money was exactly what the immigrants lacked. They found it through selling illegal liquor and, in some cases, by supporting other illegal activities. As Gladwell writes, "Crime was the means by which a group of immigrants could transcend their humble origins. It was the 'crooked ladder' of mobility."

This book tells the story of the Market as it was told to me by Steve Polski. It is meant to be a legacy for his family and a tribute to his father, Willard, who groomed Steve to own the Market, beginning only a few years after Steve's birth in December 1948. Not much has changed since then—or maybe it has.

Before we delve in, first let me share one of my own memorable experiences dining on ribs at the Market. It was an early Sunday night in March 1962, the same day I left town for Fort Leonard Wood, Missouri, to begin my basic training in the U.S. Army. I was to leave that evening by train from the Great Northern Depot, now the site of the Federal Reserve Bank of Minneapolis, located on Hennepin Avenue adjacent to the Hennepin Avenue Bridge spanning the Mississippi River and across the street from the main post office. (The post office is still there today, and a newer version of the bridge still spans the river.) Even though my tour of duty was for only six months and I would be home for a two-week leave following my basic training, my mother insisted on hosting a farewell dinner for me the night of my departure. She chose the newly opened Market Barbecue at 28 Glenwood Avenue North[3] since it was only minutes from the depot. What a great farewell! I devoured a full slab of the hickory-smoked ribs along with a large dish of coleslaw and a baked potato. I did add a little hot sauce to the meaty ribs, which gave them a bit of a kick. You could easily tell how much I enjoyed my "last supper." The evidence was all over the front of my shirt. Those ribs were the best send-off a soldier ever had.

Following my army stint, I returned to Minneapolis and, like so many of its customers, have been a frequent guest and all-time fan of the Market ever since. So, when Steve Polski approached me about writing the story of the Market, shortly before Thanksgiving in 2013, my curiosity was peaked. I wondered, though, how much could actually be written about the place. What kind of history was there? It didn't take me long to find out. Steve and I met for lunch at the restaurant and I listened to him regale me for several hours with just a taste of the stories about the Market's origins and his family's role in it. I was convinced there was an important chronicle to tell. In fact, I was so captivated by Steve's stories that I forgot to eat. I went home hungry, not just for those tasty ribs, but to begin working on this incredible story about the Polski family and the restaurant, or rather institution, they created. I have done my best to verify the facts surrounding the stories you will read in this book, but much of it is necessarily anecdotal. I hope you will enjoy reading it as much as I have enjoyed writing it.

---

[3] The restaurant opened at that location just a few months prior to that farewell dinner. It had been operated from a different location since 1946.

MARKET BAR-B-QUE

CONFIDENTIAL

Hyman Polski, probably age twenty-five

1 In the Beginning

Our story begins at the start of the twentieth century. Chaim Krasnpolski arrives in St. Paul in 1905—a world away from Poland. At twenty-one years old, Chaim is looking for a new and better life. He changes his name to Hyman Polski, meets and marries Tillie Fineberg, and raises three sons. Willard is born in 1914, Sam in 1915, and thirteen years later baby Perry joins the family.

Hyman is short in stature at under 5'3", but is barrel-chested and strong. He works as a tanner, converting animal skins to leather. It's a good guess that Hyman, while still Chaim, learned his trade before immigrating to the U.S. According to the 1921 Leather Trade Rating Book,[1] he's working for an outfit called Leather and Finds at 346 Robert St. in St. Paul. As a company salesman, he often travels to Chicago on business.

Life has become markedly better for Hyman since leaving Poland, but it still isn't easy. He can barely support his family with his meager earnings as a tanner. So in 1925, Hyman decides to leave the tannery business and opens the Cedar Street Market House, a meat and grocery store at Eighth and Cedar in downtown St. Paul. The store's main source of income is selling meat at wholesale prices to restaurants. One of Hyman's regular customers is Jacob Fredgrant, owner of a nearby restaurant who buys supplies at Hyman's store.

---

[1] *Leather Trades Rating Book: A Directory.* Shoe and Leather Mercantile Agency. Boston, MA, 1921,

One day in early 1926, Fredgrant walks into the store with a friend, Clarence Bradfield. Fredgrant introduces him to Hyman. Bradfield tells Hyman that he's an electrician and that he and several other men are planning to build a miniature distillery and are looking for investors. The cost of building a distillery is about $12,000. Bradfield invites Hyman to become part of the group and to invest in the enterprise. Hyman is well aware that building a distillery is illegal. In 1925, everyone knows about Prohibition and the Volstead Act.[2] The last thing Hyman and his family need is for him to get in trouble with the law. He

Sam and Willard

doesn't hesitate in telling Bradfield that he's not interested in getting involved in any kind of illegal business. But Bradfield persists and assures Hyman he has nothing to worry about, because he, Bradfield, is very close with General Rhinow, who heads up the Prohibition agents in St. Paul.[3]

"Rhinow will make sure nothing happens to us," Bradfield assures Hyman.

"Let me think it over for a couple of days," Hyman responds.

---

[2] The law that bears the name of Andrew Volstead, 7th District Congressman from Minnesota, formally titled the National Prohibition Act, was enacted to carry out the intent of the Eighteenth Amendment to the U.S. Constitution, which made the sale of liquor illegal in the U.S.

[3] General Walter F. Rhinow was in charge of all state troops, including the Minnesota Home Guard. His authority extended to supervising the Prohibition agents who enforced the Volstead Act. General Rhinow was a well-known figure in Minnesota.

Bradfield and Hyman shake hands, and Bradfield leaves.

Hyman wonders just how profitable a "still" could be. Since he's barely breaking even in the grocery store, he's willing to consider anything that could help his growing family live a better life. Once he discovers that a distillery could generate up to several thousand bucks a week, Hyman changes his mind. He's in. The only barrier is the $12,000 investment. Neither Hyman nor Bradfield has that kind of money. Hyman isn't about to sell his store, but he has an idea and proposes it to Bradfield.

"I'll help raise the money you need to build the still. If I'm successful, I'll sell my grocery store and invest whatever I get out of the sale into the project. If this works, I want an interest in the still."

Bradfield readily agrees to Hyman's proposal and promises him a one-seventh interest in the enterprise.

Hyman spends the next couple of months raising money. He drives over to Minneapolis to visit his friend Louis Wiggins, who owns a soft drink parlor at 323 South Third Street, not far from the Milwaukee Depot in downtown Minneapolis. Wiggins has experience in the liquor business and knows that operating a distillery could be quite profitable, but he's also concerned about the risk. Hyman assures him he has nothing to worry about, telling him that Bradfield is an undercover agent for General Rhinow. That piece of information is all it takes to convince Wiggins to join the group.

"I want to be a part of this deal," Wiggins tells Hyman. "I can invest about $4,000 to $5,000. How much money can you put in?"

"To tell you the truth, Lou, I really can't afford to put any money in right now. Later on, if things look good, I'll sell my grocery store and invest some of the proceeds into the deal. Right now, I think I can raise some additional cash from my friend Maurice Ruben. He's in the meat business and once asked me if I'd sell my grocery store to him. But the guy lives in Chicago, and I can't afford to go down there to see him."

"If you think there's a good chance this man will invest in the business, I'll pay for your trip to Chicago."

"Well, I can't guarantee you that he'll invest, but I know he has money. I think once I tell him about Bradfield, and that there is absolutely no risk in getting involved, he'll want in on the deal."

With Wiggins' support, Hyman drives to Chicago to meet with Ruben to try to persuade him to invest in the proposed venture. Ruben is hesitant, just as Hyman was when he first heard Bradfield's proposal. But when Hyman explains Bradfield's relationship with General Rhinow, Ruben changes his mind and agrees to invest $2,000 to $3,000.

Hyman asks Ruben if he knows anyone with the skills to build the distillery. He doesn't, but maybe Ruben's friend Charles Olin can help. Hyman calls Olin, who introduces Hyman and Ruben to Charles Geller. Geller has never built a distillery but thinks he could do it. But, he adds, "I'm not interested in doing anything out of Chicago, particularly not in another state."

Hyman tells Geller about the Bradfield–General Rhinow connection. Though still hesitant, Geller agrees to come to Minnesota with Ruben when Hyman and Bradfield find a proposed location for the distillery to take a look at it.

Hyman returns to St. Paul and reports to Wiggins what transpired in Chicago. With Ruben in, and Geller a possible contractor, Wiggins, Fredgrant, and Bradfield begin the search for a location. They find a farm for rent four miles from Rosemount, Minnesota, in Dakota County. It's remote enough to be a perfect site to build the still. They secure a lease for the property from Charles Stock, the owner of the farm, and Ruben and Geller travel from Chicago to St. Paul to meet Bradfield and look at the proposed site. Over lunch at the Majestic Restaurant, Bradfield convinces them they're protected by his relationship with General Rhinow, and they agree to move ahead and build the distillery.

Since Hyman doesn't know anything about building a distillery, his role is to serve as a chauffeur, conveying parts and people back and forth from St. Paul to the farm in his blue, two-door Buick coach.

On October 15, 1926, Hyman picks up Ruben and Geller at the St. Francis Hotel in downtown St. Paul and drives them out to the farm. As they drive through the gate to the distillery, Hyman spots a man standing outside the farmhouse pointing a shotgun directly at his car. He stops the Buick, but he and his two passengers, who are sitting in the back seat, remain in the car. The man with the shotgun approaches the car and orders everyone out, telling them to line up next to the farmhouse. That man is Herman Schroeder—a Prohibition agent. Hyman, Ruben, and Geller do as they're told and line up next to the farmhouse. A few minutes later, another car drives into the farm carrying General Rhinow and several other Prohibition agents. They arrest Hyman, Ruben, Geller, and the other men at the distillery, including Clarence Bradfield. All are charged with conspiracy to avoid the Volstead Act (also known as the National Prohibition Act) and with violating the Eighteenth Amendment to the U.S. Constitution.

According to the United States District Court files[4], the "feds," otherwise known as Prohibition agents for the Fourteenth Prohibition District, got wind of the distillery from an informer. That informer was Clarence Bradfield.

On the day following the arrests, October 16, 1926, the headline on the front page of the *St. Paul Pioneer Press,* printed in bold, black letters, reads:

DRYS SEIZE 70,000 GALLON STILL, JAIL SIX

"Drys" was a shorthand way of referring to the Prohibition agents. It was, more broadly, the term used to describe anyone who supported Prohibition. Those opposed were called "wets."

---

[4] I was able to obtain these files from the National Archives under the Freedom of Information Act.

On November 2, 1926, a grand jury indicts each of the eleven co-conspirators, including Hyman and Clarence Bradfield, for violating the Volstead Act[5]. Each is released pending their trial by posting a $5,000 bond guaranteeing their appearance at the trial. Hyman's bond is posted by Anthony and Abraham Fineberg, presumably relatives of Hyman's wife, Tillie Fineberg.

Prior to the trial, Bradfield files an affidavit with the court identifying himself as an informer for the Prohibition agents. His affidavit states that prior to meeting with Hyman Polski at his grocery store, Bradfield was contacted by an individual who wanted to hire him to help install some electric motors to be used in the operation of a distillery. He reports this to Major B. B Wilcox[6], who's in charge of the St. Paul Prohibition agents. Wilcox instructs Bradfield to accept the job and to let him know where the illegal distillery is located and when it's ready for use, so his agents can raid the distillery and then destroy it. Presumably the October 15 arrest of Hyman and his cohorts at the distillery site is a result of Bradfield "blowing the whistle" by contacting Major Wilcox and telling him it's time for the raid.

The case proceeds to trial on November 21, 1927, and on December 3, 1927, the jury finds Hyman, Jacob Fredgrant, Charles Geller, Maurice Ruben, and Harry Skar guilty as charged. Lawrence Jenson, Henry Lotfog, and Charles Stock are acquitted on all counts. The verdict does not mention Ledgerding, Wiggins, or the informer, Bradfield. Presumably the charges against these three men were dismissed following their indictment.

An affidavit filed before the trial sheds some light on the role anti-Semitism in the Twin Cities may have played in this scenario. It was filed by Charles Stock, one of the eleven defendants indicted

---

[5] Clarence E. Bradfield, Jacob M. Fredgrant, Charles Geller, Lawrence Jenson, William Ledgerding, Henry Lotfog, Hyman Polski, Maurice Ruben, Harry Skar, Charles J. Stock, and Louis B. Wiggins.

[6] Presumably, Wilcox reported to General Rhinow.

in the conspiracy and the owner of the farm where the distillery was located. Excerpts from Stock's affidavit, dated October 26, 1926, just days before the grand jury indictment, explain that:

"...on or about August 11, 1926, two Jewish men...came to his farm located ... northwest of Rosemount, and asked him to rent the farm ... One was a Jewish looking man ...; the other Jew ...

On August 12th the Jews again appeared ... the two Jews mentioned agreed to pay affiant ..."

How much this description of Hyman and the other Jewish men charged with the crime had on the court and the jury is impossible to ascertain. It's also impossible to know whether Mr. Stock intended to use the words "Jewish" or "Jew" in a pejorative manner or simply as a description of the men. However, what is beyond dispute is that anti-Semitism was rampant in Minneapolis at the time of Hyman Polski's trial. As the American journalist Carey McWilliams pointed out in a piece written in 1946, "Minneapolis is the capitol of anti-Semitism in the United States."[7] Interestingly, McWilliams goes on to point out that this does not include St. Paul and distinguishes the Twin Cities in this regard.

Each of the five convicted conspirators, including Hyman, is sentenced to two years at the federal prison at Leavenworth, Kansas. However, they appeal their convictions to the Eighth Circuit Court of Appeals in St. Louis. Their lawyers argue that Hyman and his cohorts were set up by Bradfield through his deal with the Prohibition agents, and that as a result, they were entrapped into building the distillery. While the Court of Appeals does not dispute the facts, it rules that this does not constitute entrapment under the law. On July 6, 1929, the court affirms the decision of the District Court and orders Hyman and his co-defendants to begin their two-year sentence at Leavenworth.

---

[7] Carey McWilliams, "The Curious Twin," *Common Ground*, September 1946.

But the lawyers aren't quite finished. They file one more appeal to the courts—this time, they file a petition for a Writ of Certiorari with the United States Supreme Court. This procedure allows a defendant dissatisfied with the outcome in the Court of Appeals to ask the Supreme Court to review the ruling. It is up to the Supreme Court to determine whether it will hear the case. That's the good news for Hyman. The bad news is that the Supreme Court has total discretion as to whether or not to hear the case. Unfortunately, for Hyman and his co-defendants, The court is not persuaded to hear the case and rejects the writ. At this point the legal process is complete, and there is nowhere for Hyman to go but to jail. He finally arrives at Leavenworth on December 29, 1929, to begin his two-year sentence.

Now more than two years have passed since Hyman was found guilty of conspiring to violate the Volstead Act. It is unclear what he did during this time period. Presumably, he sold the grocery store after raising enough money to build the distillery, and used the proceeds of the sale to purchase his interest in the enterprise. However, being faced with a prison sentence could not have made finding work easy. According to Leavenworth hospital records completed by Hyman when he began his prison sentence, he describes his occupation as a salesman. Perhaps he returned to work as a tanner following his initial conviction.

The prison hospital records also describe Hyman as forty-four years of age, five feet three and a half inches tall, weighing 166 pounds, and having a pendulous abdomen. The records indicate that Hyman continued to believe he was framed. According to the report from the prison chaplain's office issued the same day as the hospital report, when asked to provide the reason for the act leading to his imprisonment, Hyman responded: "Did not do nothing."

Clearly, this must have been a very difficult time for Tillie, Hyman's wife, and for Willard and Sam, Hyman's two oldest sons. Son Perry was only two years old when Hyman began his prison sentence. Willard was

Hyman Polski's mug shot as he entered Leavenworth Penitentiary on December 29, 1929

fifteen. He was forced to quit school and go to work to help support the family. Sam, aged fourteen at the time, remained in school and graduated from high school. It would be seventeen years before these brothers opened the restaurant we know as the Market Barbecue. While it's unclear what kind of work Willard was able to find without a high school diploma at the onset of the Great Depression, it's clear that the Polski family was in very bad shape financially. The loss of Hyman's earning power had to be a major blow to their well-being.

2 Early Release

Hyman remained in prison for less than a year. Beginning in March 1930, just a few months into his sentence, several letters were sent to the Leavenworth Parole Board requesting his early release. On March 1, 1930, the president of the Elk Laundry Company in St. Paul wrote the following letter to the parole board:

> "...Mrs. Polski... has asked that I [write you] regarding [Mr. Polski's] character..., which I am glad to do... if it might aid in bringing about his early return to a family that is certainly in very great need of his support. For more than ten years as head of the Minnesota Leather Company[1] he sold leather and various kindred supplies to [Elk Laundry] ... [W]e found him absolutely honest and trustworthy ... His ultimate failure in this line was due to economic conditions over which he had no control.
>
> It was in a more or less desperate attempt to quickly regain the heavy losses of years that moved him to do the thing that led to his present difficulty... In this matter he was ill advised... yet considering the situation fairly I do not find it difficult to be a little charitable and likewise sympathetic, particularly [because] he was facing the loss of his home."

A similar letter was sent to the parole board dated March 12, 1930, by Mr. N. Gordon, owner of the N. Gordon Company, which

---

[1] Was Hyman the "head" of the Minnesota Leather Company? He definitely worked for the company, but there is no evidence that he was in charge.

sold leather findings and shoe store supplies. Mr. Gordon told the parole board he has known Hyman for twenty years as both a friend and an employee.

In a undated letter to the parole board presumably sent around the same time, Louis Hertz, a resident of St. Paul, wrote:

> *"Mr. Polski until convicted and imprisoned had a good repu-tation, and had never been involved in any trouble before that time. His family is destitute. Their home was sold by mortgage fore-closure..."*

On May 26, 1930, Milton Rosen volunteered to be Hyman's "First Friend or Advisor," if he was granted parole. This Statement of commitment, submitted on an official form, is required by Leavenworth and used to determine whether or not to grant an inmate parole. Rosen identified himself as being in the business of selling automobile tires for the Milton Rosen Tire Company. [2] In the letter, he states that he has known Hyman for ten years. The letters and the Statement of Friend or Advisor led to Hyman being granted parole, and on December 11, 1930, he was released from Leavenworth to return to Tillie and his three sons in St. Paul more than a year earlier than expected. Although the St. Paul City Directory of that year indicates that he resumed his original profession as a leather and shoe finding salesman, it's more likely that he initially worked for the Milton Rosen Tire Company.

---

[2] Rosen many years later became a St. Paul City Council member and "took on" Professor Mulford Q. Sibley, a prominent member of the faculty at the University of Minnesota, in a controversial debate. Sibley often put forth arguments for positions that he didn't support but believed were proper subjects of discussion at an academic institution like the University of Minnesota. When he wrote a letter to the *Minnesota Daily* advocating that the university should allow a nudist club, free love, and the teaching of communism, Rosen challenged him to a debate. It took place in January 1964 and was broadcast statewide. Lehmberg, Stanford F., *The University of Minnesota, 1945–2000*. University of Minnesota Press, 2001.

A year later the city directory lists Hyman's employment as being with the Hungarian Grill, a restaurant located at 1 West Ninth Street in downtown St. Paul. The owners are Hyman and his brother-in-law Abr (Abraham?) Fineberg. Presumably, this is the same "Abraham Fineberg" that acted as surety, along with his brother Anthony, following Hyman's indictment in 1926. Hyman was also listed as an owner, though it's doubtful whether he contributed much to the purchase price, given his adverse financial circumstances following his release from Leavenworth. Perhaps his wife Tillie's brother, Abraham, provided him with the necessary cash. Other than selling supplies to restaurants when he ran the Cedar Street Market House, this appears to be Hyman's first foray into the restaurant business. The Hungarian Grill had a very short life span. By 1932, the St. Paul City Directory shows the property as being vacant.

However, this is the beginning, not the end, of Hyman's involvement in the restaurant business. In 1932, following the closing of the Hungarian Grill, he opened Polski's Kosher Style Restaurant, the House of Good Food, at 136 East Sixth Street, between Robert Street and Jackson Street. It remained open into 1935. Willard, who was about eighteen when the restaurant opened its doors in 1932, went to work there for his dad. It was his entrée into the restaurant business.

The restaurant was established at the height of the Depression—not the most auspicious time to establish a new business. Many people couldn't afford to buy a meal at Polski's Kosher Style Restaurant or, for that matter, at any other restaurant. But Hyman turned no one away. While providing free meals didn't help Hyman's bottom line, it did make the restaurant increasingly popular. One day an Englishman came into the restaurant looking for a meal. But he wasn't looking for charity.

"Can I do some work for you to pay for my meal?" he asked Hyman.

"What did you do in England? How did you make your living there?" Hyman replied.

"I worked in a restaurant as a waiter."

"Well, congratulations. You're now a waiter at Polski's Kosher Style Restaurant," Hyman told him.

The Englishman turned out to be the best waiter Hyman ever employed. One day, one of the restaurant's regular customers told Hyman that he could no longer eat at the establishment.

"Why not?" Hyman asked him.

"Well, I love your restaurant. The food is fabulous, and the service is even better. But I can't afford to tip the waiter the nickel he deserves."

Despite his best efforts and loyal customers, by 1936, the restaurant was forced to close. Not too surprising, given the difficult economic situation, but not good for Hyman and his family.

In the following two years, the St. Paul City Directories list Hyman's occupation as a peddler. In 1938 he's listed as a "buyer," but his son Perry[3] says that Hyman "became a cattle dealer, driving a small truck around the state, buying a cow or two from a farmer, selling them to a place like Armours [sic], and, in a word, being on the road most of the time. Periodically, he returned to our home [at 740 Dayton Ave.], and it was on such a trip he died." Perry believes that his father died from a combination of kidney failure and a severe asthma attack.[4] This was on May 9, 1938, just two days before Perry's eleventh birthday. Hyman was fifty-two.[5]

---

[3] Perry, the younger brother of Willard and Sam, has never been involved with the Market Barbecue. He has made California his home for well over half a century.

[4] Hyman's death certificate lists the cause of death as pulmonary edema.

[5] Hyman's widow, Tillie, would live another fifty-one years, passing away on February 21, 1989, at the age of ninety-nine years and eleven months.

3 The Next Generation

After Hyman's death, the family's financial situation became even more desperate. Willard's contribution to the family coffers helped, but it was too small to make much of a dent in their depressed economic situation. Willard needed to find a better paying job, so he and his brother Sam moved to Minneapolis, settling into a small unit at the Oak Grove Apartments near Loring Park. Perhaps there were more opportunities in the bigger city, but Willard's lack of a high school diploma and the fact that neither brother had any formal vocational training made the search difficult. To make matters even worse, large numbers of skilled workers who had lost their jobs due to the Depression were also looking for work.

Two additional factors came into play in Minneapolis: anti-Semitism and Jewish mobs. Anti-Semitism was rampant throughout the Midwest at the time, but especially in Minneapolis. Historian Laura Weber summarized the situation in the following terms: "... Minneapolis has a dark past with respect to its attitude toward Jews and employment, a difficult era that lasted from the end of World War I until a number of years after the conclusion of World War II. Its peak occurred during the Great Depression..."[1] She goes on to describe the rise of organized anti-Semitism in the city:

---

[1] "Gentiles Preferred: Minneapolis Jews and Employment, 1920–1950," *Minnesota History* 52 (Spring 1991), 167, 172.

Minneapolis began to come out of the worst effects of the depression by 1936. Economic improvement was evident there in most categories by June, 1935, and in all areas by June, 1937. Improvement in economic conditions, however, did not bring about a decline in job discrimination and other forms of anti-Semitism in Minneapolis. It was 1936 when William Dudley Pelley's Silver Shirts, a fascist hate group, first actively attempted to recruit members in the Twin Cities. The group made enough of an impact to become the subject of a six-part investigation in the Minneapolis Journal *in September of that year. The reporter was Arnold Eric Sevareid, fresh from the University of Minnesota, much later to become famous as a network television newscaster. According to Sevareid's reports, the group claimed 6,000 members in Minnesota with 300,000 nationwide. One of the aims of the local group was to segregate all Jews in one city in Minnesota. "Anti-Semitism is the outstanding feature of the Silvershirts [sic]," Sevareid wrote. In the late 1930s help-wanted ads could still be found in Minnesota newspapers stating "Gentile" or "Gentile preferred."[2]*

Meanwhile, Hyman Polski had not been the only one trying to exploit the economic benefits generated by bootlegging. Two Jewish mobs had surfaced, each making a fortune selling illegal booze and running illegal gambling activities. One was headed by Isadore Blumenfeld, aka Kid Cann, and the other, known as the Syndicate, was led by Davie Berman.

Davie Berman was born in Odessa, Russia. His father was a rabbinical student and a violin player who came to the United States to avoid being conscripted into the Russian army. After he settled in North Dakota, his wife and children joined him. Davie's father didn't do well there and the family eventually moved to Sioux City, Iowa, where Da-

---

[2] Reprinted with the permission of the Minnesota Historical Society.

vie's gangster career began. Following the ratification of the Eighteenth Amendment and the enactment of the Volstead Act, Davie owned several illegal distilleries and began to develop a network of workers who helped him change the economic fortunes of his family dramatically. Later, Davie and his brother Chickie moved to Minneapolis, where Davie developed a close relationship with Mayor Marvin Kline. With Kline and the local police looking the other way, he ran and eventually controlled the largest gambling operation in Minneapolis.

Willard, age fourteen

With this backdrop, the Polski brothers were desperate to find jobs that would pay a living wage. Willard met Chickie Berman, Davie Berman's younger brother, who ran Davie's gambling operations in downtown Minneapolis, and the two hit it off immediately. Chickie offered Willard a job running a crap game on Hennepin Avenue, in downtown Minneapolis. Presumably, Sam found similar employment through Chickie.

Running a crap game was not for sissies; violence often accompanied the gambling. To help Willard in his new job and to make sure only the "right" people were let in to play craps, Chickie hired Rocky Lupino as the doorman. (This is the same Rocky Lupino who grew up in northeast Minneapolis, spent time in prison for kidnapping Tony DeVito in St. Paul, and may have been involved in the 1946 bombing of Stouffer's Restaurant in downtown Minneapolis. He committed suicide in 1962 while serving time in a Missouri prison.) Not only did this new line of work increase Willard's standard of living and help out his family, it also led to a life-long friendship with Chickie.

In 1941, Willard's wife, Anne, gave birth to their first child, a girl they name Loraine. One day, shortly after Lorraine and Anne came home from the hospital, Chickie stopped by to meet the new baby. Chickie and his wife had long wanted children, but were unable to do so. As Chickie laid his eyes on Loraine for the first time, he was completely charmed. After gazing at her for a few minutes, he reached into his pocket, pulled out ten hundred-dollar bills, and placed them on the table in front of Willard.

"Willard, here's a thousand bucks. I want to buy your daughter."

Willard paused for just a second and then responded, "Chickie, I work for you, but I can't sell you my daughter."

Chickie was serious about his offer, but that was the end of it. While he and his brother Davie were ruthless in their gambling activities, they were both very loyal to their friends. Willard was not just Chickie's employee, but was also his friend. Loraine remained with her parents, and Chickie never brought up the subject again.

Willard being visited in the hospital by starlet Dolores Moran

4 The War Years and Beyond

When World War II broke out, the Polski brothers were still working for the Bermans. The Depression was over and money was flowing. But duty called. In 1943, at age twenty-nine, Willard enlisted in the U.S. Army. He was assigned to Camp McQuaide, near Watsonville in Santa Cruz County, California. The camp served as the West Coast Processing Center for the Army and the official stockade for stateside Army AWOLs and other troublemakers.

Shortly after arriving, Willard was on night maneuvers and fell, injuring his back. While in the base hospital, he was visited by Dolores Moran, a pin-up girl and a fledgling movie star. A picture of her visit with Willard appeared in the local newspaper. Following Willard's release he received a medical discharge, and by the end of the year he was back in Minneapolis, a civilian.

Meanwhile, Sam also joined the Army. He was assigned to the quartermaster corps and was stationed on the island of Tarawa in the Pacific Ocean, where he was put in charge of mass burials of casualties. He remained at Tarawa until the war in the Pacific ended, returning to Minneapolis in 1945.

With the advent of war, Davie Berman's focus changed. He was more interested in killing Nazis than in running a gambling empire. His obsession with and hatred toward the Nazis had begun long before the U.S. entered the war in December 1941. Referred to as "Davie, the Jew," he was active in opposing Nazi rallies in Minneapolis. In an article published by the American Jewish Historical Society titled "Jews in America: Jewish Gangsters," we learn about his pre-war activities:

> In Minneapolis, William Dudley Pelley organized a Silver Shirt Legion to 'rescue' America from an imaginary Jewish-Communist conspiracy. In Pelley's own words, just as 'Mussolini and his Black Shirts saved Italy and as Hitler and his Brown Shirts saved Germany,' he would save America from Jewish communists. Minneapolis gambling czar David Berman confronted Pelley's Silver Shirts on behalf of the Minneapolis Jewish community.
>
> Berman learned that Silver Shirts were mounting a rally at a nearby Elks' Lodge. When the Nazi leader called for all the 'Jew bastards' in the city to be expelled, or worse, Berman and his associates burst into the room and started cracking heads. After ten minutes, they had emptied the hall. His suit covered in blood, Berman took the microphone and announced, 'This is a warning. Anybody who says anything against Jews gets the same treatment. Only next time it will be worse.' After Berman broke up two more rallies, there were no more public Silver Shirt meetings in Minneapolis.

Once the U.S. entered the war, Davie was eager to enlist in the Army and fight the Nazis in Europe, but the Army wouldn't accept him. A convicted felon, Davie had served time in Sing Sing Penitentiary on a kidnapping conviction. Under U.S. law, a convicted felon is not eligible to enter the armed forces. But that didn't stop Davie. He traveled to Winnipeg, Manitoba, and enlisted in the Canadian Army. Offered a commission, he turned it down. He wanted to fight Nazis, and he wanted to fight them in the trenches. Assigned to fight in Europe as a lance corporal, he was badly injured at the Battle of Anzio. He received a medical discharge and returned to Minneapolis in 1944.

Following Davie's enlistment in the Canadian Army, his brother Chickie enlisted in the U.S. Army. He became a first lieutenant in the Medical Corps and he, too, was injured—by a land mine in North Africa in 1943. He also received a medical discharge and returned to Minneapolis.

So when Willard returned to Minneapolis after receiving his medical discharge, he found that both Chickie and Davie Berman were busy fighting the Nazis in Europe, and he couldn't return to his job running a crap game. He found work for a brief time with the A. O. Smith Company, a manufacturer of hot water heating equipment. From there he went to work in the Minnesota Knitting Mills shipping department, which at the time was located on West Seventh Street in St. Paul. Ted Kueller, whose father owned the business at that time, remembers Willard as being likeable but very tough, and with a lot of anger. He recalls that Willard held a very low-paying position. But despite his not making much money, Willard's family continued to grow. His second daughter, Bonnie, was born in August 1944.

At war's end, Sam and Willard were back together in Minneapolis, both needing permanent jobs. You might think that employers welcomed veterans, but you would be wrong, especially if the veterans were Jewish. Anti-Semitism was still rampant in Minneapolis. Jews were excluded from country clubs, the Minneapolis Athletic Club, and the Minneapolis Club. Jews couldn't even join the Automobile Club. Jewish doctors were excluded from practicing in hospitals—a situation that led to the establishment of Mt. Sinai Hospital in 1948. Jewish lawyers were forced to form their own law firms.

> *... Minneapolis is the capitol of anti-Semitism in the United States... In almost every walk of life, 'an iron curtain' separates Jews from non-Jews in Minneapolis... So far as I know, Minneapolis is the only city in America in which Jews are ... ineligible for membership in the service clubs ... Jews have never been accepted for membership in the local Kiwanis, Rotary, Lion, or Toastmasters organizations... Even the Automobile Club refuses to accept Jews as members.*
>
> *Many concerns in Minneapolis, notably some of the chain stores and Montgomery Ward & Company, pursue a general policy of not interviewing Jewish applicants...*
>
> *The most significant aspect of anti-Semitism in Minneapolis, however, consists in the lack of significant Jewish participation in the dominant economic activities of the city. In milling, lumbering, transportation, private utilities, banking, insurance, and... Department-store merchandising, Jews do not figure as an important element...[1]*

None of this boded well for Willard and Sam. And the prospect of returning to the gambling industry suffered a blow when Hubert Humphrey was elected mayor of Minneapolis in 1945. Humphrey ran against Marvin Kline, who had been mayor since 1941, on a campaign to clean up the city. Davie Berman was a great supporter of Kline, and Kline, in turn, turned a blind eye to the Berman Syndi-

---

[1] Carey McWilliams, "The Curious Twin," *Common Ground*, September 1946.

cate's gambling enterprise, enabling them to become the gambling overlords of Minneapolis. Kline's defeat spelled the beginning of the end for the Berman's gambling enterprise. Although Humphrey only partially succeeded in cleaning up the city, he did get rid of gambling and prostitution and ultimately made Minneapolis a more livable city. Although Kid Cann and his mob continued to control the sale of liquor in Minneapolis, Davie Berman saw the writing on the wall and moved to Las Vegas, where he partnered with East Coast gamblers to transform what had been illegal operations in Minneapolis into a legitimate business in the desert of Nevada.

David and Chickie Berman

Davie Berman retained his connections to the Jewish mob scene throughout his life, but the move to Las Vegas gained him respect and even adoration in his new community. He had completed his climb up the rungs of the "crooked ladder." Like Hyman Polski, he died young, at age fifty-four. In 1957, Davie underwent routine surgery to remove a polyp from his colon and died on the operating table. But unlike Hyman, who didn't live long enough to reach his goal of respectability, Davie Berman did. His story is told by Susan Berman, Davie's only child, in her 1981 book, *Easy Street*.[2]

Chickie moved to Las Vegas with his brother, but he stayed there for only a few years before moving to Lewiston, Idaho. When Davie

---

[2] Susan Berman, *Easy Street*, The Dial Press, 1981.

died in 1957, his wife, Gladys, went into shock, became ill, and never fully recovered from the loss. As a result, she was in no condition to take care of Susan, who was twelve when her father died. Chickie was also stunned by his brother's death. The two had always been close. When Chickie learned that Gladys was no longer able to care for Susan, he brought her to Lewiston to live with him, his wife, and their two adopted children, Donna and Dave.

Meanwhile, back in Minneapolis, the Polski brothers, both married, spent their days and evenings hanging out. Willard and Sam, like many war veterans, became "rounders"—a term used for someone who likes to drink and gamble and hang out in bars. They played pool at the Lincoln Rec on Hennepin Avenue, went to bars, but what they loved most was to play cards. Gin rummy and pinochle were their favorites.

Even with Davie Berman in Las Vegas and Hubert Humphrey cleaning up the gambling scene in Minneapolis, Willard and Sam managed to land jobs running a bingo game in Elk River, a small town about thirty-five miles northwest of Minneapolis. It's unclear who their boss was. Perhaps the game was a remnant of the Syndicate's gambling empire.

The Market Café was located at 130 North Seventh Street, close to the old Minneapolis Farmer's Market at the edge of downtown. The address no longer exists, but if it did, it would be in the shadows of the Target Center.

5 The Market Café

Always on the lookout for a place to hang out and play cards, Sam found a small breakfast spot called the Market Café for sale located at 130 North Seventh Street, close to the Minneapolis Farmer's Market at the edge of downtown. The Farmer's Market was thriving, and a number of small businesses had opened shops nearby. A number of them were housed in a single structure built in the nineteenth century that today we would call a strip mall. Many shared identical first names. Along with the Market Café, there was the Market Barbershop, a one-seat haircut joint; the Market Cigar

Store; and Molly Segal's Fruit Store. Other local businesses included Gunnar Fagero's Butcher Shop with its floor covered in sawdust, Sutton's Bar, and the First Produce Bank Building. Across the street stood the Gorham Building, home of the infamous *Minnesota Line*. That newspaper, which was launched in the late 1940s and published by Leo Hirschfield, is reputed to have originated the system of placing odds on a sports bet. Prior to the *Minnesota Line*, the only bet you could place was whether a team would win or lose.

Patrons walking into the Market Cigar Store would have seen six stools in front of a bar where they could sit, relax, and smoke a cigar. Behind the bar was a floor-to-ceiling blanket separating the front of the store from the back room where fifty card tables were set up. There were typically at least a hundred guys back there smoking and gambling. It was a very attractive place for Willard and Sam to satisfy their card-playing obsession.

The Market Café served only breakfast. The main floor was an L-shaped room with seating for ninety customers. It had a small counter that seated six along with eleven booths and four tables. The small kitchen and bathrooms were also on the main floor. A basement had been added by digging out the limestone base of the building, and there was a small second floor with a six-foot ceiling used for storage and for the pot-bellied stoves that heated the building. Deliveries were made through a dumbwaiter constructed in the sidewalk outside the building.

The café looked like both a good business and a good opportunity to Sam Polski. In 1946, he purchased it from Jack Segal and assumed the lease with the owners of the building at a cost of $300 a month. Sam got the money he needed to buy the café from his friend Forbes Simon. Forbes became half-owner, though he wasn't involved in the day-to-day operations of the café. While Willard had no ownership interest in the Market Café (at least not yet), he could often be found there whenever he had the time to drop by. While the brothers still wandered over to the Market Cigar Store to play cards occasionally, they no longer had to scrounge around to find a place to play. There was always a table available to them at Sam's Market Café.

The brothers' euphoria was short-lived, however. As much as Sam loved the Market Café, it wasn't a money-maker, barely generating enough business to cover the monthly rent. The location was good, but there just wasn't enough business to support a breakfast place. Most of the guys who hung out in the neighborhood were rounders like Willard and Sam. They liked to play cards, smoke cigars, and stay up late, and seldom got up early enough in the morning to eat breakfast. Willard and Sam were just the same, often looking for a place to have a late-night snack. They loved barbecue and often satisfied their hunger pains at late-night rib joints such as Peggy's Barbecue or the Plantation.

Meanwhile, Willard's gig running the bingo game in Elk River came to an end, and he found himself right back where he started—in desperate need of money to support his family. Sam's situation wasn't much better. He owned the Market Café but was losing money on the venture. About the only good thing about the café was that it guaranteed an open table for him and his brother to play gin rummy.

Willard and Sam began to think that maybe the Market would do better if it opened later, stayed open late, and served ribs instead of eggs. They figured if barbecue worked for Peggy's, why not for the Market Café? Sam felt he had nothing to lose. Even if a rib joint wasn't successful, he'd be no worse off than he was now running a coffee shop. Either way, there would still be a place for Willard and him to play cards.

When Sam started to convert his breakfast café to a late night rib joint, he saw an opportunity to have Willard join him in the business. He could provide Willard with a job, the brothers could work together, and equally important, they could continue to play cards together any time they chose.

Forbes Simon had been doing Sam a favor when he became his partner in the Market Café; he was never involved in its operation, and Sam had no difficulty buying his stake for the original price of $2,500. Sam then made Willard his equal partner, and within a year Willard had repaid Sam the same amount from his share of the profits from the new, and immediately successful, Market Barbecue.

6 Another New Beginning

The Market Barbecue didn't open until late afternoon and didn't get busy until after the bars closed and the downtown rounders came looking for a place to eat. It didn't close until the last customer was done eating, no matter what time in the early morning. For their first cook, the Polskis hired Fisher, who most folks called Big Fish because of his portly body. He, along with Willard and Sam, developed the barbecue recipes. From the first, the ribs were prepared in a large brick pit over an open wood fire, just as they are today. Lulu and Anita were the first waitresses, and George Schwartz, who went by the name of Watts and lived on the half-floor above the restaurant, was hired as the night watchman. Willard's brother-in-law Dick Mark became the bouncer. To save money, the only phone on the premises was a pay phone. When Willard or Sam wanted to call home, they'd place the call from the pay phone and hang up after one ring. That was a signal to their families to call back. They'd do anything to save a dime!

Both brothers dressed to the nines at work. Each spring Willard bought two new suits from Juster Brothers Clothing Store—one brown and the other black. He wore brown or white shoes with the suits, depending on the season. In the fall he returned to Juster's to buy two dark-colored suits for the winter.

Though Willard and Sam were only fifteen months apart in age, and were about as close as two brothers can be, there were a lot of physical differences. Willard was almost six feet tall, weighed about two-hundred pounds, and had hazel eyes and auburn hair (it would turn gray and eventually fall out as he aged). Sam looked more like Hyman. He was only five feet seven and built like his father—short and stocky. He had a receding hairline and wore glasses. A scar on the top of his head was a reminder of the day Hyman hit him with a bench. As a young man Sam had a brief career as a professional boxer. Willard's son Steve, who took over the Market from his father in 1976 (and who provided much of the information for this book) says his Uncle Sam reminded him of Terrence Aloysius "Slip" Mahoney, the Leo Gorcey character in the Bowery Boys movies.

Willard was much more of a hands-on guy than Sam. He involved himself in all the details of running the Market, from cooking in the kitchen to keeping the books to being in charge of the dining room and its customers. He had an amazing memory for names and never forgot a face that came into the Market. Sam, on the other hand, preferred to play the role of an executive. He did greet customers, but otherwise was happy to let Willard do the manual labor required to run the restaurant.

Willard and Sam's favorite activity was gambling. They would bet on anything. One warm summer day they took Steve and their much younger brother Perry to Bridgeman's Ice Cream Shoppe on Sixth and Hennepin, a short walk from the Market Barbecue, for an ice cream cone. As they approached Bridgeman's, the brothers noticed a car attempting to parallel park in front of an adjacent business. They stopped to see if the driver would be successful.

"I'll bet you five hundred bucks he doesn't make it," Willard said to Sam.

"You're on," Sam quickly replied.

It's not clear who won the wager and whether the loser paid. But when they finally entered Bridgeman's and started paying for their ice cream cones, the brothers got into a serious argument over how to pay for Perry's fifteen-cent cone. Which one will pay a dime and which one a nickel?

Arguing was a part of the brothers' DNA. They could and did argue over almost anything. One day Willard bragged to Sam about how far Steve could throw a baseball.

"Oh, I can throw a ball farther than he can," Sam responded immediately.

"Prove it," Willard said. "I bet you a hundred bucks Steve has a better arm than you do."

The next morning Willard and Steve met Sam at Fern Hill Park near their home in St. Louis Park for a "who-can-throw-a-baseball farther" contest. Steve, age thirteen, beats Sam, age forty-seven, and Willard's net worth increased by one hundred dollars.

7 More Than a Restaurant

This first incarnation of the Market Barbecue was definitely not a family restaurant. It was a rough place and began to get crowded during a rough time of the evening. (Steve remembers his father telling him that in the late 1940s more people were walking around downtown at Seventh and Hennepin in the evening than at noon on a Saturday in the 1970s.) In the late 1940s, vets returning from the war wanted to go out, see shows, have drinks, and were always looking for fun. The Market didn't have a liquor license, but that didn't stop customers from drinking in the restaurant. If they didn't bring their own bottle with them, they could usually buy one from a vendor hanging around outside nearby. The restaurant chipped in by selling "set-ups" in addition to food: one glass of ice went for two bucks. Because the Market stayed open until five in the morning, it attracted a lot of seedy characters, including nice folks who had had too much to drink, prostitutes, and gangsters.

Although consuming alcohol in the restaurant was illegal, the police usually looked the other way. When the police did stop by, Willard and Sam always treated them with special respect and offered them discounts—free coffee and half-price food off the menu. Not surprisingly, the Market quickly became a gathering spot for the police—so much so that the restaurant was often referred to as the "North Side precinct." The city even passed an ordinance providing that only two police cars could be parked in front of the Market at any one time. Again not surprisingly, the ordinance was not strictly enforced.

You could find Willard and Sam at the restaurant at almost any time of the afternoon or evening. When they weren't working, the brothers sat in a booth playing cards. They also used the premises as a place to bet on sporting events. Even though the brothers argued between themselves, if anyone else so much as uttered a bad word about either brother, the other one would jump to his defense. This

Sophie Tucker

was especially true of Sam, who had once been a professional boxer—he took no lip from anyone.

Almost immediately the Market began to attract celebrities. The Twin Cities were home to numerous nightclubs and theaters, among them the Club Carnival on Fifteenth and Nicollet, across the street from the current address of the Market; the Pick-Nicollet Hotel on the corner of Hennepin Avenue and Washington Avenue; the Orpheum Theater on Ninth and Hennepin; and across the river in St. Paul, the Lowry Hotel, to name just a few. They attracted a top line of celebrity performers with two things in common: none of them like eating before a performance, and all of them were ravenously hungry once they were done.

The Market was the perfect place for them. Bob Hope, Sophie Tucker (the "red hot mama"), Perry Como, and Liberace are just a few of the many stars who satisfied their hunger pains with late-night meals at the Market. For many years Liberace and his brother George send Willard a Christmas card that included a 45 RPM recording of their music that could be punched out of the card. Autographed photos of many of these stars still crowd the walls of the restaurant today.

About the same time that Sam Polski's breakfast café morphed into the Market Barbecue, another now-famous restaurant appeared. Art and Marie Murray, owners of Murray's Red Feather Cafe and Bar in the Russell Hotel at 18 South Fourth Street, purchased a building at 26 South Sixth Street, closed the Red Feather, and moved their restaurant to the new building. They changed the name to Murray's Restaurant and Cocktail Lounge. Both the name and location are the same today.

The Red Feather Cafe and Bar remained vacant until Willard and Sam decided to open a second location in around 1950. They rented the space and changed its name to the Pit. The brothers agreed that Sam would run the new restaurant while Willard remained in charge of the Market.

The Pit was much larger than the Market. It was really more of a nightclub than a restaurant. Boasting an elevated stage lined with pinball machines, it was a perfect spot for Willard and Sam to satisfy their gambling craze. Hundred-dollar bets were placed regularly in their ongoing pinball tournaments. There was also a large back room which provided a perfect venue for gambling. That room was almost always full. The Pit sold a lot of liquor, but the food they served was brought over from the Market, where a lot more ribs were consumed. On a daily basis the Market would sell 160 to 320 slabs of ribs compared to 32 at the Pit, whose customers were more interested in drinking and gambling than eating.

All of this tended to make the Pit an even tougher place to manage than the Market. The Pit attracted more criminal types. According to Steve, *Crime Digest* published an article describing how rough a place the Pit was. Sam's boxing ability helped keep customers in line, but even he became overwhelmed by the responsibility of maintaining some semblance of order. Finally, after less than three years of operation, the brothers decide to find a new location for the restaurant. Looking for a site that was smaller and more manageable, they moved the Pit to 300 South Third Street, previously home to Jack Doyle's Chicken Shop. Although the new location was a few blocks away from the Russell Hotel, the neighborhood was just as rough, and the same problems continued. Handling the Pit's clientele became too much even for Sam. They might have stuck with it if business was booming, but the Pit's receipts were substantially less than the Market's. By the end of 1956, Willard and Sam decided to close the Pit. The brothers had had enough of running multiple restaurants. One Market Barbecue was enough for them.

8 A Surprise Change of Venue

Willard and Sam assumed that they'd continue to run the Market from its location at North Seventh Street forever. The rent was affordable, and the landlords seemed happy to have them as a tenant. But soon they learned that nothing lasts forever. In 1961, from out of the blue, they received a termination notice. The landlords had decided the property would generate more income as a parking lot than as a strip shopping center.

Willard and Sam were stunned. The only conversations they've ever had with the landlord had been about renovating the property, not about tearing it down. While they expected rent increases once the building was updated, they figured the Market would also attract more customers. Instead, they realized they were about to lose their only location, and with it the customer base they'd developed over the last fifteen years.

The brothers begged the landlords to postpone the demolition and let them continue to operate the Market until they could find a new location. The landlords were not sympathetic, agreeing only to extend their lease for two more months and increasing the monthly rent to $1,000—more than a three-fold increase from what they'd been paying. It was hard to swallow the huge increase in rent, but the landlords gave them no choice. They needed to find a new location, and they needed to find it fast.

They began looking for a new location, well aware that they

The Market at its 28 Glenwood Avenue location

couldn't afford any gap from the time they closed the Market at its current location to a reopening somewhere new. Luck was with them. Less than block away, the Wiseman Candy Warehouse Building at 28 Glenwood Avenue was available. Abe and Paul Wiseman, the owners of the property, were moving their business and were looking for a buyer for their warehouse. Although the location was good, the building's physical condition was not. It would cost the brothers $55,000 to renovate it. Could the business possibly support such an expense? Willard and Sam weren't sure, but they knew they had no other option. Time was running out. If they hesitated, they'd still be forced to close the North Seventh Street location, and with nowhere to relocate, they'd lose their customer base. The brothers decided to bite the bullet and take over the Wiseman Candy Company warehouse.

The ground floor of the warehouse was larger than what Willard and Sam needed for the Market. (The second floor was rented out to various small businesses.) Willard's brother-in-law Hank Sabes expressed interested in opening a bar in the portion of the building the Market didn't need. Sabes, who also owned South of the Border and the Key Club on the corner of Washington and Fourth Avenue South in downtown Minneapolis, wanted to expand his empire. His brother-in-law, Herb Klein, who ran the liquor operation at the Point Supper Club in Golden Valley, wanted to move downtown. The excess space in the Wiseman Candy Company warehouse was the perfect size for the bar Herb wanted to open. Sam, Willard, Hank, and Herb agreed to join together to purchase the warehouse. But since Hank Sabes was married to Willard's sister-in-law, Willard didn't think it was a good idea for him to have any ownership interest in the building. Besides, Hank Sabes was a controversial figure in Minneapolis,[1] and the parties agreed that any interest Hank had in the ownership of the property should not be visible, so Sam and Herb Klein (who was "fronting" for Hank Sabes) agreed to purchase the Wiseman Candy Company warehouse from Abe and Paul Wiseman.

The brothers borrowed $55,000 from the First Produce State Bank to fund the required renovations, and the Market moved from 130 North Seventh Street to 28 Glenwood Avenue in late 1961. Customers poured into the new location, and within a year the brothers had repaid the $55,000 bank loan in full. Meanwhile, Herb's Bar opened in the adjacent space with an interior door connecting the two businesses. Herb's almost immediately became a popular spot, but it didn't serve any food, so after an evening of drinking, the bar's customers were looking for somewhere nearby to eat—good news for the Market.

The Glenwood Market was larger than the one on Seventh Street. Two dining rooms stood back-to-back, separated by a narrow hall-

---

[1] In 1951 Sabes was said to be a partner in the American Sales Service Co., which sold vending and slot machines, the latter of which were illegal in Minnesota. In February 1957 a fight led to Sabes shooting and killing musician Charles M. Talley. It was deemed self-defense.

way. The front room seated seventy-five customers, the rear eighty-five. Booths lined the perimeter of the front dining room with tables filling up the interior space. The rear dining room was open only on weekend nights after midnight. It had no booths, only tables, and was used primarily for card playing. A third room in the rear of the building housed meat coolers and an ice machine, with additional storage space in the basement. Red, yellow, and brown tiles covered the floor of the front dining room, while the rear dining room floor was covered in brown tiles. The kitchen was located on the right-hand side of the restaurant as you entered the building. It was roughly eight feet wide and twenty-one feet long. There was a dishwashing and food preparation area immediately behind the kitchen. Curtains were painted on the windows. (Anything to save a buck!)

The local police never bothered Willard and Sam about the gambling in the back dining room. Perhaps they were unaware of it—no money was visible. The only items on the table in addition to the cards were a pad of paper and pencil for keeping track of the results. Willard and Sam made book with their customers at the end of each evening unless they didn't trust the integrity of a card player. In that case, the player was required to put up his money before playing. But even then, the money stayed in Willard's or Sam's pocket, not on the table.

9 Willard's Family Expands

The Market took up most of Willard's time, but not all of it. In December 1948, Willard and Ann's third and last child, Steve, was born at St. Joseph's Hospital in St. Paul. Willard finally had the son he'd always wanted. It's not that Willard didn't love Loraine and Bonnie; he loved them both dearly. But Willard had always dreamed of sharing the Market with one of his children and he didn't think it was an appropriate place for his daughters (or his wife, for that matter) to hang out.

Shortly after Steve was born and Willard became Sam's partner in the Market, the family moved from St. Paul to St. Louis Park. A backyard gate led directly into Chickie Berman's backyard. Willard and Chickie were still good friends, and Chickie was Steve's godfather (perhaps a concession by Willard after refusing to sell Loraine to Chickie seven years earlier). Steve remembers waking up in the morning as a small child and running out the back door of his house and through the gate leading to the Bermans' house. He didn't want to be late for breakfast with Chickie, where bacon was often served—a delicacy he never got to eat at home. Even though the Market Barbecue specialized in pork ribs, Steve's mother maintained a kosher home. Bacon never appeared on her table.

Steve's early life revolved around Willard, Willard's gambling, and the Market Barbecue. Steve describes his childhood as being like growing up in a "Goodfella" world. Although his family wasn't involved in crime like Henry Hill and the Lucchese crime family in the

Above: Steve coming through the gate leading to Chickie Berman's house
Below: Willard and Ann Polski with children Steve, Loraine (center), and Bonnie

movie, crime was all around them. Chickie Berman was their back-yard neighbor. Willard's best friend was Bixie. (While Steve is sure "Bixie" is a nickname, he never heard him referred to by any other name, first or last.) Bixie was a loan shark. He provided his customers with high-interest loans (one percent a day) to cover their gambling on sporting events. The exorbitant interest (known colloquially as "vigorish") that Bixie collected on these loans allowed a more than comfortable standard of living. He was never seen without his German shepherd and a .45 pistol tucked under his shirt. While Bixie was not a large man, it was a mistake for anyone to confuse his size with his power. This was especially true for anyone who failed to make a timely loan repayment. He could be quite ruthless collecting the "vig" due him—something immediately apparent to the borrower when he felt the cold steel of Bixie's .45 on his neck and saw the sharp teeth of a large dog snarling at him.

Like most of Willard's friends, Bixie was also a veteran of World War II. After being stationed in the Pacific, he returned home with a collection of money from the Philippines, Japan, and other countries in the South Pacific. When Steve accompanied his dad to visit Bixie, Bixie gave Steve a wallet-full of foreign currency.

Bixie's life came to an abrupt end when he was shot in the back of the head while playing gin rummy in the basement of the Pit Barbecue one day in 1954. The presumed assailant, of course, was an unhappy debtor. According to Steve, Bixie's dead body was placed in the back seat of his Buick, which had a white interior. When Bixie's brother arrived to pick up the body and discovered blood all over the back seat of Bixie's car, he became upset for the first time.

Another of Willard's friends was Georgie Brooks, part owner of the Flamingo Hotel in Las Vegas and partner of Davie Berman. Georgie showed up in Minneapolis a couple of times a year in his pink Lincoln Continental Mark III. He and Willard were fishing buddies, and they frequently brought Steve along on their outings. The routine is

The Willard Polksi family plus Willard's mother, Tillie

always the same. Willard and Steve hop into the Mark III and Georgie drives them to Monticello to fish in some of the lakes near the Mississippi River. When they arrive, Georgie parks his car and, rain or shine, changes into a solid green outfit—pants, shirt, and hat. They're out on the lake all day, and they always catch plenty of sun fish, crappies, and perch. At the end of the day, Steve has a stringer of fish to take home.

"Where are you going with those fish?" Georgie always asks.

"I'm going to put them in the trunk," Steve replies.

"You're not putting those stinking fish in my car!"

So Steve dutifully throws away the catch. Each time Steve goes fishing with his dad and Georgie, history repeats itself. No fish ever come home with them. Kind of like the bacon at Chickie Berman's.

Another one of Willard's pals was Papa Joe Mancino. Papa Joe owned the Town Pump Bar at 801 Marshall Street N.E. on the east side of the Mississippi. Whenever Willard was looking for a good deal on just about anything, from a suit of clothes to a set of golf clubs, he went to Papa Joe. Willard took Steve with him on some of these buying trips. Like fishing with Georgie Brooks, the routine was always the same. Willard tells Papa Joe what he wants. Papa Joe then goes into the phone booth at the Town Pump and places a call. About five minutes later, Papa Joe comes out of the phone booth, tells Willard how much the item will cost and where to pick it up. His "source" is his brother Tony, who runs a fencing operation out of the trunk of his Cadillac El Dorado. Depending on the day of the week, his merchandise includes shoes, men's suits, tennis rackets, golf clubs, and numerous other items.

Steve loved meeting his dad's friends. He loved going places with Willard. But his dad also made it clear to him that there were some things that were none of his business. Steve learned this the hard way when he was twelve. He was washing his dad's 1961 blue Mercury Monterey convertible. Wanting to do a thorough job, Steve opened the trunk to wipe up any water that might have seeped in. Willard spotted him opening the trunk and came running out of the house, slammed the trunk shut, and yelled at Steve,

"NEVER, EVER OPEN THAT TRUNK AGAIN!"

Inside the trunk there was a case of whiskey, bottled in pints, that Willard planned to sell to customers at the Market, even though the restaurant had neither a bar nor a liquor license.

In looking back at his childhood, Steve describes it as being "the best of times and the worst of times."

10 Steve and the Market Meet

By the time Steve was ten, Willard was bringing him regularly to the Market at 130 North Seventh Street. Their typical routine was to stop first at the First Produce State Bank, on the corner of First Avenue North and North Seventh Street, where Willard did his banking. From there, the two would continue down the block to Gunnar Fagero's butcher shop. Steve loved going there. He liked the sawdust that covered the floor and especially enjoyed the piece of sausage Gunnar always handed him. The next stop on the tour was the Market Cigar Store. Too young to smoke, Steve nevertheless enjoyed the aroma of the tobacco. From the Market Cigar Store, Willard and Steve went on to Molly Segal's Fruit Stand, where Molly always handed Steve a nice piece of fresh fruit. Finally, they arrived at the Market Barbecue. Willard took Steve into the kitchen, where Fisher was waiting for them. Fisher would cut off a single rib from a full slab and hand it to Steve in a napkin. Steve chewed on it as if it were a lollipop.

This was the fun part of going to the Market with Dad. But Steve was also introduced to the seamier side of the restaurant. He frequently noticed people bringing in clothing, golf clubs, tennis racquets, and other items, which they offered to sell for much lower than retail prices. Steve wondered where all the merchandise came from. When he asked Willard about it, the answer was always the same:

"They fell off the back of a truck."

It seemed to Steve that his dad has decided to go into competition with Papa Joe's brother, Tony. (Such dealings will have an impact on Steve many years later at the Market's Glenwood Avenue location.)

When the Market moved to 28 Glenwood Avenue, Steve helped his dad by removing the booths from the Seventh Street store to install at the new location. He begged his father to take the five potbelly stoves from the small second floor that were used to heat the Market Café before Sam bought it in 1946, but Willard refused. He didn't want to lug them over to Glenwood, even though it was no more than a block away. Willard did take the large "MARKET BAR-B-Q" sign that had hung above the entrance at North Seventh Street to the new location, but once there it never saw the light of day. Willard deposited the sign in the basement where it remained until the Glenwood location was demolished to make way for the Target Center many years later. The marquee at the front of the Market today is based on that sign.

Young Steve at about the time he started visiting the Market

The Market wasn't the only thing Willard shared with Steve. Willard loved baseball and nurtured this same love in his son. Willard played catch with Steve and took him to the Minneapolis Miller baseball games. Before the Washington Senators moved to Bloomington in 1961 to become the Minnesota Twins, the Millers were the only game in town. (In 1936, the Millers became a farm team of the Boston Red Sox. In 1938, the New York Giants bought the team, and the Millers became a farm team of the Giants for the next nineteen years. The Giants moved to San Francisco at the end of the 1957 season. The

Red Sox then resumed ownership of the Millers for the last three years of their existence.)

The Millers played their home games at Nicollet Park in South Minneapolis until 1957, when that stadium was demolished. The Millers then moved to the newly completed Metropolitan Stadium in Bloomington, which would become the home of the Twins in 1961. Their arch rival was the St. Paul Saints. The Saints, a farm team of the Brooklyn Dodgers and later the Los Angeles Dodgers, played their games at Lexington Park.

Many Miller ballplayers became regular customers at the Market. It wasn't unusual for Willard to return home in the evening after closing the Market accompanied by one or more of the players, like Bill Taylor, Don Great, Gene Bordeaux, or Babe Barna. While Willard wasn't much of a drinker, he had plenty of booze at home for these late-night guests. The players had a few drinks, passed out, and spent the night at the Polskis'. In the morning, Steve would meet the ballplayers while Willard served them breakfast. Later, Willard would drive them to the ballpark for that day's game.

When Willard wasn't sitting in Met Stadium watching the Millers, he was listening to the ballgame on his car radio. Once, when Steve was seven and riding in the car with his dad, Willard drove him to the highest spot he could find so they could find out the results of a San Francisco Giants game that Willard had placed a bet on.

Frank Buetel, who was the sports director at WTCN-TV (Channel 11 today) for twenty years and later spent three years as the voice of the Twins on television, was also a regular patron at the Market and a good friend of Willard's. A huge baseball fan, Buetel often brought Steve baseball memorabilia, including a ball autographed by Ted Williams. That autograph is especially significant to Steve since Williams played for the Millers before joining the Boston Red Sox in 1939.

One very early morning in 1961, when Steve was twelve, Willard came into his bedroom, turned on the light, and woke him up.

"Steve, I want you to meet someone. I want you to meet someone," Willard repeated excitedly.

Steve opened his eyes, and at the end of the bed standing next to his father was Moose Skowron, the great first baseman for the New York Yankees.

Steve's uncle Sam was also an important part of his early life. The two families always got together for holidays. Sam's daughter, Sheryl, was a couple of years older than Steve, and his son, Howard, was two years younger. The cousins played together at holiday gatherings. Sam gave Steve a few boxing lessons in the basement at the Market, and those lessons later inspired Steve to become a "golden glover." He also took lessons from Eddie Lacy and Jerry Glover at the Pillsbury Settlement House. Steve enjoyed competing, but his career came to an end when he was invited to fight one of the inmates at the state prison in Stillwater. Steve was a senior in high school at the time. He declined the invitation and hung up his gloves forever. He had more important things to do, like starting college at the University of Minnesota.

11 Steve's Market Career Begins

By the time Steve turned thirteen, he was working as a dishwasher on Friday and Saturday evenings at the Glenwood Market. His hours started at midnight and ended at four in the morning. Two years later, after he got his driver's license, he began training as a cook on Monday and Tuesday evenings, learning the recipes, how to take inventory, and how to control the pit. Once Steve had enrolled at the University of Minnesota, his duties expanded to include cashiering and serving as the Market's maître d', as well as its bouncer. His hours didn't change; he started work around midnight and finished about four or five in the morning. Not only did this help Steve learn various aspects of the business he would eventfully own, but it gave him further opportunities to spend time with his dad.

As Willard became aware of how well Steve was able to run the restaurant without him, he became comfortable spending more time in the rear dining room playing cards, especially after midnight. It wasn't unusual for Steve to wait for his father to finish a card game before the two drove home together. Late nights became a regular part of Steve's life, especially on weekends.

On one of those evenings in the middle of a Minnesota winter, an attractive woman came into the restaurant clad in a long fur coat and approached Steve.

"I'm looking for Willard. Is he around?"

"He's busy right now. May I ask why you want to see him?" Steve responded.

"I have a message for him," she said with a broad smile.

"Please wait here, and I'll see if he can be disturbed."

Steve went to the back room where his father was engaged in a serious card game. He was reluctant to interrupt, knowing that will only anger Willard, but felt he had no choice.

"Dad, can I interrupt you a second?"

"Steve, for Christ's sake, you know better than to interrupt me when I'm in the middle of a card game. Please leave me alone."

"Sorry, Dad, but there's a woman who wants to see you. She says she has an important message for you."

"I don't give a good goddamn! Tell her I'm busy and can't be disturbed."

Steve wisely chose not to press the point; he returned to the front room and spoke to the woman waiting in her fur coat.

"I'm very sorry, but Willard can't be disturbed right now."

"OK," she replied, "but maybe you can deliver the message for me."

She unbuttoned her coat and opened it wide so Steve could easily see that there was nothing but bare flesh underneath.

"Wish your father a happy birthday!"

On another late evening when Steve was in charge of the restaurant, a man came into the Market and identified himself as "John from Des Moines." He told Steve he was looking for some action. Steve excused himself to go into the rear dining room to get Willard. This time Willard agreed to see what was going on.

"Hello, sir. My name is Willard Polski, and I'm one of the owners of this place. What can I do for you?"

"Like I told the kid here, I'm looking for some action."

He then pulled out $55,000 in cash and laid it out on the table. Willard quickly swept the money up, gave it back to John from Des Moines, and led him away to the rear dining room. John sat down at a table across from Three Finger Kleve, and the two played cards into the early morning. Willard later had a chance to find out more about John from Des Moines, and discovered that John had recently been released from Attica Prison in New York, where he'd been serving time for pulling out a sawed-off shotgun and pointing it at a highway patrolman.

Steve enjoyed working at the Market despite the late nights. Just being able to be with his father on a daily basis meant a lot to him. The only problem was when Willard and Sam disagreed about something. Although the brothers would defend one another from any third party, that didn't prevent them from squabbling between themselves. When that happened, Sam's trump card was to threaten to fire Steve. While Sam never followed through on that threat (and Willard wouldn't have let him even if he wanted to), it made life at the Market a little less comfortable for Steve.

One evening, when Steve was still in high school and working one weekend day at the Market, the phone rang. He answered: "Market Barbecue. May I help you?"

"Yes. I'd like to place an order to go. I'm staying at the Radisson Hotel. I'd like five orders of chicken and five orders of ribs. Can you deliver them to me at 3:30 this afternoon?"

"Sure."

The caller is Elston Howard, the famous catcher for the Yankees and the first African American to be on its roster.

Normally, a take-out order is delivered by cab, but not this time. Steve tells Willard, "Dad, I'm going to deliver this order myself."

He takes the order to the Radisson where he's greeted by a bellboy.

"I'll deliver the order to Mr. Howard."

"No thanks. I'm delivering this myself," Steve informs the bellboy.

He goes to the room, knocks on the door, and Elston Howard answers it dressed in his underwear. Steve looks in the door and sees Mickey Mantle, Roger Maris, and Whitey Ford, all in their underwear, chasing girls around the room.

12 A New Generation of Owners

In 1970, after Steve finished college and completed a short stint in the Army, he began to work full-time as manager of the Market. In 1976, when Willard turned sixty-two and became eligible to receive Social Security benefits, he sold his 50 percent ownership interest in the Market to his son, receiving payments from Steve in installments. Steve began working sixteen- to eighteen-hour days, arriving home in the early morning. With Steve getting home so late, Willard tried to help out by continuing to open the restaurant every morning. He was supposed to arrive at about ten o'clock, but usually showed up a couple of hours earlier. This arrangement didn't always work the way Steve would have liked, however. Early one morning Steve was still sound asleep when the phone rang. Steve groggily answered the call.

"Steve, you left the light on in the basement," Steve heard his dad telling him.

"So, turn it off, Dad. The whole point in your opening up is so I can get some sleep."

Business continued to go well. Willard and Sam were still playing cards, but Steve was now in charge of the business. The only other change was that Sam finally stopped treating him as just another employee and gave up trying to fire him.

Meanwhile, Sam's son, Howard, who had also worked as a dishwasher at the Market when he was in high school, returned to Minneapolis after spending two years in the advertising business in Chicago and New York. He began working full-time at the restaurant and became co-manager along with Steve. Around 1980, Howard acquired his dad's interest in the Market, making him and Steve equal partners. The cousins ran the business together, with Howard assuming more day-to-day responsibilities.

In enjoying more delicately smoked meats, I've made a recent discovery that's sort of a reversal of the gin-and-charcoal phenomenon.

For about as long as I've been in Minneapolis, there's always been a Market Barbecue, and it's always been understood that the Market Barbecue is one of the reliable places to stop late at night, after a night on the town, to stow away some barbecued ribs and show your gut who is master of the situation before heading home for the night. The Market has been a particular favorite of rib fanciers who favor tight, lean, rather ascetic ribs over the fat, billowy soft kind.

But in the matter of food that is customarily consumed only is the wee hours of the morning, usually after a round of bars, a question naturally arises. Is it really good? Or is it good only in the context of middle-of-the-night, sobering up feeding, and in comparison with what else is available at that hour?

Until the Market took to opening in the middle of the day recently, to serve the downtown lunching trade, there wasn't an answer. And until the Market inaugurated its 11:30 a.m.–2:30 p.m. lunch hours, it was the first time—I suddenly realized the first day I walked in—that I was ever in the place sober.

It is a joy to report that the food tastes as good in the cold, sober light of midday as it does late at night. Maybe better.

– Will Jones, "After Last Night,"
Minneapolis Tribune, July 12, 1978

The front room at the Glenwood location

One of the first improvements the cousins made was to obtain a beer and wine license from the city. That was good news for the restaurant, but bad news for the gambling. Once Steve and Howard saw how beneficial the license could be for business revenue, they were no longer willing to risk losing it—which they certainly would do if the police ever raided the back room. That ended the open back room gambling, but not the end of card playing for Willard and Sam. They could always find a table, either upstairs or in the Market's basement.

It soon became clear to the cousins that it would be a good idea to buy the building they were located in rather than continuing to rent. In 1982, Steve and Howard approached the owners, Sam and Herb Klein, with just such a proposal. A deal was struck that included a large down payment with the balance payable over the next three years. Now Steve and Howard were the sole owners of both the restaurant and the property. In addition to no longer having to pay rent to operate the Market, the cousins began to collect rent from the businesses that occupied the second floor of the building.

When Willard and Sam owned the Market, they did virtually no advertising other than handing out business cards designed by Eddie

Schwartz. Eddie was a big fan of the Market. On November 13, 1979, he mentioned the restaurant in his weekly column in the *Skyway News*.

"LOOK BACK-WARDS... The menu is the same as 40 years ago, the decor has been changed to match that era, so now the Polski Cousins are getting the 'Back Room' in shape including new carpeting so Glenwood & Second Avenue North will never be the same again... Mpls/St. Paul mag... rated it as 'the granddaddy of all local rib places'... Now run by Steve and Howard Polski (dads Sam and Willard started the spot in 1946 across the street from my former printing plant on North Seventh Street... In our book... it's the best barbecue in Our Town."

Having spent some time working in the advertising business, Howard convinced Steve that the Market would benefit from additional marketing. One of their first initiatives was to enhance the appearance of the Market and increase its visibility from the street. To this end, they decided to install awnings on the front of the building. They hired Hoigaard's to manufacture and install the awnings and directed them to print the words "Market Barbecue" on them to make it easier for passers-by to spot the restaurant from the street. But the specialists at Hoigaard's informed Steve and Howard of a Minneapolis ordinance restricting the height of any lettering on a downtown building to two inches. Such a restriction defeated the purpose of the awning so the cousins dropped the idea.

The Market Barbecue at 28 Glenwood Avenue, complete with awnings

But one day, while Steve was still mulling it over, Lou DeMars, at that time the president of the Minneapolis City Council, came into the restaurant. DeMars had been a good customer of the Market for years, and Steve decided to share his tale of woe regarding the awnings with him.

"How large do the letters need to be?" DeMars asked Steve.

"I'm not sure, but maybe two feet," Steve replied.

"Go ahead and order the awnings, Steve."

"But Lou, what about the ordinance?"

"Steve, what's my job?"

"You're head of the city council."

"Order the awnings."

Steve did just that, and Hoigaard's installed them with "MAR-KET BARBECUE" engraved in two-foot-high letters—now easily visible from the street.

That change, as well as other renovations, did not go unnoticed. In January 1981, the following article appeared in the *Twin Cities Reader:*

> *There is a new look at the Market Bar B-Que Cafe, the corner restaurant located at Glenwood and Second Avenue North in the entertainment district of downtown Minneapolis. A fresh exterior of red brick, frosted glass windows and decorated awnings invite diners to enter. Inside, one notices new woodwork, an old-time tin ceiling, brass accessories, new carpeting, ceiling fans, and more brick—all contributing to a cozy 1940s atmosphere.*
>
> *These additions have been made without altering the charm that has made the Market Bar B-Que a Twin Cities landmark for 35 years...*
>
> *The recent facelift given to the Market has helped to make it a "trendy" place again, but the tradition of making smoked pork spare ribs over a hardwood fire in an enclosed barbecue pit will never change, according to Steve Polski. The cafe's barbecued rib specialty has made the restaurant famous even though the Polski family does not invest heavy in advertising.*
>
> *No fake sauces or charcoal flavoring are used to create the barbecue taste, just a natural hardwood smoking process. Mild or hot sauce is served on the side, but the ribs are also delicious without dressing.*

13 Branching Out to Minnetonka

Willard's and Sam's track record running multiple restaurants was poor. The Pit was not successful. As they reflected on that experience, the brothers agreed that it was just too difficult to have more than one location. They never should have opened the Pit. And while Steve and Howard were too young at the time to remember that experience, their fathers never failed to remind them, especially after the cousins became co-owners of the Market. However, several very good patrons of the Market who happened to live in the western suburbs urged the cousins to open a suburban location. One evening in 1985, the cousins were schmoozing with one of those customers, Dave Trijurnhom, and he once again suggested they were missing out on a sure bet by not opening a suburban location.

"There are a lot of rib lovers who live in the suburbs but don't like to come downtown to eat. You guys need to have a place in the 'burbs. There's a perfect location waiting for you right off of Highway 12 [now Interstate 394] just a bit east of Wayzata. Go take a look at it."

Steve and Howard figured there was no harm in looking, so they took the fifteen-minute drive from downtown to see the property. It turned out there was already a restaurant on the location, now closed, with the kitchen and tables still in the building. The property was owned by Richard Neslund, a well-known local real estate developer. Neslund built the restaurant on the property for his nephew, a former opera singer with a great voice but no experience running a restaurant.

59

The restaurant was a knock-off of the popular Perkins style, but it was never successful.

Steve and Neslund had met before when Neslund worked as a glass salesman for Steve's then father-in-law, Buddy Brin. This made the discussion a little easier for Steve. Neslund was asking $850,000 for the property. Given the family history running multiple restaurants, Steve and Howard were reluctant to buy. They told Neslund they wanted to lease the property for a year with an option to buy at any time during that first year for $850,000, with lease payments to be applied against the purchase price if they exercised their option. Neslund agreed.

The cousins hired Steve's high school friend Jim McNulty, president of McNulty Construction Company, to renovate the existing structure into a barbecue joint. They figured it would cost them $350,000 to create a 4,500-square-foot restaurant with a dining room that seated 130 people in booths and tables. They also planned to add a bar that would seat forty. For the first time, the Market would have a full liquor license where customers could purchase liquor in addition to wine and beer.

Steve and Howard were confident the new location would be a success and improve their bottom line, but in light of Willard and Sam's previous failures, the cousins wanted to make sure they crossed all their "t's" and dotted all their "i's." They organized an invitation-only grand opening on a Wednesday evening in May 1985 and sent out invitations to more than two-hundred people. Earlier that week, Carl Pohlad had come into the Glenwood Market to pick up some ribs to take home for dinner. Carl, a well-known Minneapolis banker and philanthropist, and since 1984 the owner of the Minnesota Twins, was a frequent customer of the Market. After Carl picked up his ribs, Steve, who had never said a word to Carl in the past, approached him.

"Carl, I'm opening a new restaurant in Minnetonka, and I'm having a grand opening this Wednesday at seven o'clock. Would you be interested in coming?"

Carl replied, "Thanks for the invitation. Sounds like a great party. I'll see what I can do."

Wednesday evening finally arrived and the turn-out for the opening was over the top. The place was packed with guests. It was an exciting evening, people were eating ribs, drinking hard liquor for the first time, legally, at a Market restaurant, and the

Market Bar-B-Que owners Howard Polski (far left), Steve Polski (second from right) and friends.

Market Moves West

A downtown-Minneapolis tradition is extending its hospitality to the western suburbs. The tastiest ribs in town—**Market Bar-B-Que**'s, of course—are scheduled to be purveyed this spring at 15320 Wayzata Blvd., right next to Chi-Chi's on Highway 12. Owners Howard and Steve Polski say the bar and restaurant at their new location will offer the same mouth-watering ribs and chicken you've enjoyed at the Market's Glenwood Avenue "headquarters." Watch your newspaper for the new Market's opening date!

A notice in *Mpls./St. Paul Magazine* announcing the opening of the Minnetonka location

noise level was deafening. Early in the evening, Steve needed a break from the tumult so he stepped outside and lit a cigarette at just the moment that a limo pulled up in front. The doors of the limo opened and out stepped Carl Pohlad and his wife, Eloise. To say Steve was surprised would be an understatement; he never expected that Pohlad would actually show up.

"Carl, how good of you to come tonight. Please come in and join the party."

The Pohlads were the hit of the evening and were among the last to leave. As Steve shook hands goodbye with Carl and watched him and his wife being driven off in their limo, he thought to himself, *Definitely a good omen for our new place.*

And Steve was right. The evening was a preview of coming attractions. The restaurant was an immediate success, with customers standing in line for lunch and dinner for the first 148 days. Steve and Howard traded off managing the Glenwood and Minnetonka locations. On the Friday evening following the grand opening, Steve was on duty. The place was packed. There was a two-hour wait for a table. The hostess greeting the guests took their names and assured them they will be seated as soon as a table became available. Steve, standing behind her near the bar, was silently reveling in the restaurant's success when he was approached by a good-looking man dressed in a sport coat.

"Are you the boss?" the man asked Steve.

"Yes, I'm the owner, but the hostess is in charge of seating."

"How long is the wait?"

"Well, how long did the hostess tell you is the wait?"

"Two hours."

"OK. How long have you been waiting?"

"I've been waiting about thirty minutes."

"Well, I'm sorry. It's probably going to be another hour and a half before a table will open up for you. You know we just opened here on Wednesday, and we're extremely busy. We're doing the best we can."

"That's not good enough," the man responds.

"Well, like I said, I'm sorry. There's nothing I can do about it. We're taking people's names. We're seating them in the order they arrive. As soon as your table's ready, we'll be happy to seat you."

"No, that's not good enough. I'm here with my wife and daughter and we expect to be seated NOW!"

"Sir, I don't know what else I can tell you."

"Fuck you!"

He grabs Steve by the throat. They're standing at the entrance to the crowded dining room filled with suburbanites trying to enjoy their meals who can't help seeing and hearing what's going on.

Steve thinks to himself, *I can't allow this guy to keep choking me, but I also can't get into a fight with him in this dining room. All these nice folks who are eating are going to choke on their food, and I'll never see them again. The people in line waiting for a table aren't going to stick around if there's a fight. I'm about to have a disaster on my hands if I don't do something quick.*

Steve figured he has about thirty seconds to decide how to respond to the jerk. His short stint as a golden glove boxer and the time he served in the Army taught him how to take care of himself. He kneed the guy in the groin, put him into a full nelson, dragged him outside, and threw him into the bushes. The man's wife and daughter came running after him, called Steve an animal, and hit him with their purses.

"You're calling me an animal? Your husband started choking me."

They continued to hit him with their purses.

"Ladies, you better back off or you're going to end up in jail."

That did the trick. The women backed off, and the three of them left. As Steve walked back into the restaurant, six customers stood up and walked out, saying, "This place is too rowdy and we don't want any part of it." But then two other customers came up to Steve and told him they saw everything that happened.

"If you want us to be witnesses, we'll be happy to give you our address and phone number. You did the right thing. That guy attacked you."

Steve thanked them, shook their hands, and went into the bar for a much-needed shot of whiskey. Although Steve never drank when at work, tonight was different. He thought to himself, *You know, I've been downtown for twenty-five years, and I never got jumped. And the third day I'm out here, supposedly with nice people, I get choked.*

Steve had no idea who the guy was and never saw him again.

Business continued to thrive at the Minnetonka location. Before the end of the first year, Steve and Howard exercised their option to purchase the property and received a $25,000 credit for their previous lease payments. The National City Bank provided the financing for the purchase.

Business was also good at the downtown location, and Steve and Howard continued to rotate between the two restaurants. Minneapolis cops continued to hang out at the Glenwood store, getting free coffee and paying half-price for ribs or whatever else they choose to eat. Things just couldn't have been rosier. Then, in 1987, a series of unrelated events occurred that would have a major impact on Steve and the Market.

Just as Willard and Sam had bought clothing and other items at a discount through Willard's good friend Bixie, Steve and Howard also received a discount on many of their purchases. Bixie was no longer around, but the Glenwood store continued to attract a lot of shady characters, including jewelry thieves, gamblers, and burglars. It wasn't unusual for people to come into the Market with something to sell since the restaurant was full of potential buyers. One individual showed up almost daily trying to sell something, anything, to Steve and Howard.

"Do you want to buy a cashmere sweater for ten bucks? Do you want to buy an Armani suit for a hundred bucks?"

The deal on the Armani suits was too good to pass up. Both Steve and Howard bought one. What the cousins didn't know was that the seller was working for the police. He had been caught in another robbery and had made a deal with the police that they would reduce the charge against him if he brought in some downtown businessmen who were involved in these crimes. One morning the police showed up with search warrants at both Steve's and Howard's homes. They knew exactly what to look for because the guy told them about the suits he'd sold Steve and Howard. The cousins were arrested, charged, and convicted of committing a gross misdemeanor. The Market's liquor license in Minnetonka and its wine and beer license downtown were revoked for thirty days, and Steve and Howard were each sentenced to thirty days in the Minneapolis work/release program. Both restaurants remained open and continued to serve food during this period.

Just as Hyman Polski, Steve and Howard's grandfather, had been set up by Prohibition agents fifty-eight years earlier, Steve and Howard were now set up by the Minneapolis police. While history had seemingly repeated itself, the price paid by Steve and Howard for getting caught was substantially less than the one paid by Hyman.

14 Howard Bows Out

Another issue was lurking in the background. It first came to light in 1979, when the city of Minneapolis expressed an interest in creating a green space around the building that was home to the Glenwood Market. City officials threatened to take the property through a condemnation proceeding, but Steve talked them out of it. The issue resurfaced, however, when the owners of the city's new NBA franchise, the Minnesota Timberwolves, decided to build a stadium on the corner of Seventh Street and First Avenue North. The arena, called the Target Center, would be within spitting distance of the Market's location on Glenwood Avenue North. The city backed the new stadium a hundred percent and agreed to construct a parking structure nearby on land where the Market and several other businesses stood. Steve and Howard received notice that the city intended to condemn their property. And this time there was no talking them out of it. This meant, of course, that once again the Market would to have to find a new home, if Steve and Howard wanted to maintain a presence downtown. As if this wasn't trouble enough, Steve's marriage was unraveling at the time, and Willard, who had been diagnosed with diabetes, metastatic bone cancer, and prostate cancer in 1983, took a substantial turn for the worse.

Encouraged by the success of the Minnetonka Market, Howard became interested in finding a third location for the restaurant. During a trip with Steve to Phoenix in 1987, a distressed piece of property had caught his eye. The cousins knew that the owner of the property owed the Internal Revenue Service a substantial amount in unpaid income taxes. Hoping to take advantage of this information, the cousins offered to purchase the property for a sizable discount from the asking price. The owner declined the offer. The next day the IRS seized the property for the back taxes, and the cousins returned to Minneapolis empty-handed.

That was fine with Steve, who wasn't much interested in having a Market so far from their center of influence, but it wasn't fine with Howard. He was disappointed, and, according to Steve, he returned home feeling depressed.

Back when Howard acquired Sam's interest in the Market in 1980, the cousins had entered into a buy-sell agreement. The agreement included a so-called "Russian roulette" provision, under which either Steve or Howard could force the sale of the other's interest in the Market by electing to purchase it. If that happened, the other partner would either have to sell at the price designated in the offer or purchase the interest of his partner on the same terms. One day in early April 1987, while the cousins were sitting at a table at the Glenwood Market, Howard triggered the provision. He offered to purchase Steve's interest for $325,000.[1] Steve was stunned by Howard's action. (Looking back on that event many years later, Steve wonders whether Howard exercised the "Russian roulette" clause because of his disappointment over not being able to find a new location in Phoenix.)

"How can Howard do this to me now?" Steve wondered. "He knows my dad is dying, that my marriage is about to go to hell in a hand-basket, and that we're being forced to find a new downtown location for the Market. What in the hell am I supposed to do?"

Steve didn't want to sell his interest. The Market was his entire life, and he had no idea what he'd do without it. To sell his interest,

---

[1] I contacted Howard Polski to get his version of this story and to obtain additional information about his father. However, Howard declined to be interviewed.

what with everything else that was going on in his life, was not the thing to do. But that wasn't Steve's only option. Under the Russian roulette clause, he could also force Howard to sell his interest for 325 grand. But the agreement also required the transaction to close within thirty days from the date the trigger was pulled, so Steve needed to make a quick decision.

Steve believed the business was worth more than the $650,000, price Howard was putting on it. If he decided to sell, he wouldn't be getting what he thought it was worth. Then again, if he decided to buy, it would be a good deal for him. But where would he get the money? Steve didn't know, but he was confident he'd find a way to complete the purchase. So he rejected Howard's offer and informed him that he was going to buy Howard out. Steve then began to search for the money.

Brian Kvasnick was a long-time customer of the Market and a good friend of Steve's. He owned Spectro Alloys, a metal company. More than once Brian had hinted that if the opportunity ever arose, he'd be interested in becoming part-owner of the Market. Steve gave Brian a call, but unfortunately, Brian was in Japan and couldn't be reached. He wouldn't be back until after the closing date on the purchase.

Steve next called his accountant, Perry Silverman, to see if he had any suggestions.

"Why don't you give Harvey Feldman a call? He owns a few restaurants around town. Maybe he'd be interested," suggested Perry.

Harvey was also a customer at the Market. More importantly, he was a good friend of Brian Kvasnick. Steve didn't know Harvey well, but well enough to ring him up. Anyway, what choice did he have? He needed the money, time was running out, and with Brian Kvasnick unavailable, his options were dwindling,

It turned out that Harvey didn't need a lot of persuading. He was interested in owning a piece of the Market and agreed to pay Steve the $325,000. Finally Steve could exhale. He was now assured of having the funds required to retain his ownership of the Market. Closing was scheduled for May 11, the day after Mother's Day.

Mother's Day is a busy day at the Minnetonka Market, and Steve was in charge. When the phone rang early that afternoon, Steve picked it up, assuming it was someone wanting to check to see if there was a waiting list for dinner.

"Good afternoon, Market Barbecue. How can I help you?"

"Steve, it's Harvey. Listen, I've been up all night thinking about our deal, and I just can't go through with it. $325,000 is a lot of money—more than I can afford to lose. I'm sorry, but I just can't do it."

"Harvey, what are you saying? My deal with Howard has to close tomorrow. If you back out, I'm going to be forced out of the business."

"I'm really sorry, Steve, I know this is a big problem for you, but I just can't do it."

"Well, can we at least talk about it in person? Can I come over?

"Well, sure. I don't think I'm going to change my mind, but I'm glad to talk to you in person. I'm over at my folks' house."

Steve wasted no time. He told the hostess on duty that he was leaving and wasn't sure when he'd be back. He drove the ten miles or so to Harvey's parents' house, all the time trying to figure out how he was going to persuade Harvey not to back out of the deal.

He arrived at the house, still not having any idea what he was going to say to convince Harvey to make the investment. Before getting out of the car, he exhaled and took a handkerchief from his rear pocket to wipe the perspiration from his neck. Steve wasn't sure if he was sweating because there was so much at stake for him in the deal, or because the temperature was 90 degrees in the shade.

Harvey and his parents were waiting for him. It was an awkward moment for Steve. He shook hands with Harvey and his father, greeted Mrs. Feldman, and sat down on the living room couch.

"Well, Steve, like I told you, after thinking this over and over, it just doesn't seem like a wise investment for me to make. I probably would go ahead with it if it just wasn't so much money."

"Harvey, I can't do anything about the amount. I need every dollar of it to buy out Howard. I know it's a lot of money, but, Harvey, it's a good investment. You'll be getting a good deal. You know I could have sold my interest to Howard for the same amount, but I'd have been giving it away. Trust me, Harvey. You're not going to lose your money. And think of the fun we'll have working together."

Steve continued throwing out all of the reasons why Harvey should become his partner. Harvey listened, but didn't say much. All of a sudden, Harvey's mother interrupted Steve in her Yiddish accent.

"Havey, du da deal!"

Whether or not Steve's arguments were effective with Harvey, they definitely worked on Mrs. Feldman. Harvey did what his mother told him to do. The next day, Harvey and Steve went to the lawyers' offices, where they meet Howard, Steve bought out Howard's interest in the Market, and Harvey stepped into Howard's shoes to become Steve's equal partner.

While Steve had survived one crisis, his marriage continued to unravel and Willard's health continued to deteriorate. On June 30, 1987, Steve received a frantic call from his mother urging him to come over to her house. Steve lived only a couple of blocks away. He found his dad in bed, obviously not doing well.

"Dad," Steve said to him, "should I take you to the hospital?"

"No, Steve. I've done everything I ever wanted to do in my life. I just want to go now."

Willard, age seventy-three, died in Steve's arms.

15 Another Move for the Market

With Howard out of the picture and Harvey in, Steve could now focus on the condemnation of Glenwood, which was heating up. How much the Market received in the deal was left in the hands of the lawyers. Steve's job was to find another downtown location. While the Minnetonka restaurant continued to do well, Steve felt strongly that the Market needed to maintain a downtown presence. His search led him to a vacant building at 1414 Nicollet Avenue. The location had previously been home to the Bowery Boys, a restaurant and bar owned by Danny Stevens, who led a band called Danny's Reasons. The restaurant was known for its oversized hamburger that two people could share like a pizza. It had been closed by the city because it had employed strippers.

Steve liked the location. He thought it would work perfectly as the Market's new downtown location. Adding to its appeal was the fact that the city was in the process of building a new convention center just a few blocks away. Steve was sure that would help the Market's business by attracting out-of-town conventioneers.

The asking price for the building was $800,000, and Steve wasn't the only one looking at it. Gary Kirt, president of Bell Mortgage, was also interested in buying the building as an investment. To avoid a bidding war, Steve and Gary Kirt worked out a deal. Kirt would buy the building and lease it to the Market. Kirt also agreed to contribute $350,000 toward the renovations required before the Market could move in. That $350,000, plus the proceeds from the condemnation of the Glenwood building, would be sufficient to fund the improvements. It all made sense to Steve as long as he could get a liquor license. But that wasn't going to be easy. All of a sudden, his gross misdemeanor conviction a few years earlier began to hang heavily over his head. Would the city agree to issue a liquor license to the Market? Steve knew that even if it did, the process would be difficult and take time. And time was what Steve didn't have. He had to either agree to the deal being offered him by Gary Kirt or continue searching for another downtown location. Steve hadn't seen all of that gambling in his life without some of it wearing off on him. He decided to roll the dice and agreed to the deal with no guarantee that the liquor license would follow.

Steve's new partner, Harvey Feldman, had a brother, also named Steve, who was a contractor. The partners hired Steve Feldman to do the renovations. Part of the work involved constructing a bar room in the front of the restaurant—though they still didn't have a liquor license. Steve had bought the so-called San Francisco bar from the recently closed White House Restaurant in Golden Valley and wanted to install it in the new bar room. Meanwhile, Brian Rice, a local attorney and a good customer, agreed to help Steve obtain a liquor license. Just as Steve suspected, it turned out to be an arduous and lengthy process, but the license was finally granted.

The new location was the largest downtown Market yet. In addition to a main dining room, filled exclusively with booths and seating for a hundred, there were two private dining rooms. One, the Coke Room, seated forty-five, and the other room had capacity for a hundred. The bar room was immediately to the right of the main dining room as you entered the restaurant. Between the bar and tables, it could accommodate an additional seventy-five guests. There was a large open kitchen at the rear of the main dining room extending the entire width of the building.

NOW THAT WE'VE MOVED WE'RE ONLY 43 YEARS OUT OF DATE.

We're not the kind of place you'll find on the strip. Our atmosphere has always been as real as our ribs. So when we moved, we were careful to keep our old wooden booths, our diner-style juke-boxes and our wall of celebrity photos. What we added were an antique African mahogany and marble bar, stocked with a full line of premium liquor, and a few other throwbacks to our distant past. You should have seen this place 43 years ago. And now you can.

1414 Nicollet Ave., Mpls. 872-1111. Complimentary valet parking available.

MARKET BAR-B-QUE ®
Real pit-smoked ribs.
T.M.

An advertisement announcing the move to Nicollet Avenue

16 Yet Another Change of Ownership

There was no way Steve could have moved the Market from Glenwood to Nicollet or, for that matter, continued to be an owner of the restaurant, if Harvey Feldman had not become his partner. And as far as Steve was concerned, the new relationship was working well. Unfortunately, it was not going so well for Harvey, who could never get comfortable in his new role as half-owner. He was incessantly worrying about the business. Was it going to succeed? Were there enough customers to support two locations? When business was good, Harvey wondered how long it would last. Finally, he sought reassurance from his good friend Brian Kvasnick. Would Brian have invested in the business if he hadn't been in Asia in 1987, when Steve needed the money to buy Howard's interest?

"Yes," Brian reassured him. "I love the Market. I'd love to be an owner with Steve."

"Well, Brian, I'll give you that opportunity. Buy me out, and you and Steve will be partners."

And Brian did just that. Less than two years after Harvey Feldman became Steve's partner, he stepped out of the business, selling his interest to Brian Kvasnick. Steve was delighted. He had always wanted to have Brian as a partner, and now that dream had come true.

The new partnership worked out beautifully. Brian was very knowledgeable about business and great with customers at the Market. Not only did he and Steve work well together managing both the Nicollet and Minnetonka Markets, they also became good friends outside of work and even vacationed together. They went to Russia; they went sapphire mining in Montana; and they searched for a lost emerald mine in Mexico.

Brian also continued to travel by himself. In 1996 he returned to Asia, where he contracted a bug that forced him to cut his trip short. By the time he arrived back home he was very sick. His doctor suspected he had pneumonia, and Brian found himself in the Southdale Fairview Hospital. Steve was very concerned and visited Brian at the hospital every day for a week. One morning when Steve called the hospital to check up on Brian, he was told that Brian had been transferred from Fairview Southdale to St. Mary's Hospital on the edge of downtown. That seemed strange to Steve. Fairview Southdale was supposed to be a good hospital.

"Why would they move Brian to another hospital?" Steve wondered. "I need to find out what's going on."

He immediately called St. Mary's and asked to speak to Brian. The receptionist transferred him to the nursing station. Again, Steve asked to speak to Brian. There was a short pause on the other end of the line. Finally, after what seemed like an eternity to Steve, the nurse responded.

"I'm sorry, sir. Mr. Kvasnick has passed away."

Steve later learned that the cause of Brian's death might have been Legionnaires' disease, a severe form of pneumonia.

Steve was shocked by the news. He had just lost a trusted partner and a special friend, and he knew he had a lot of sorting out to do. Brian was the third partner he'd lost in less than eight years. Steve was about to become the first-ever sole owner of the Market. But before that could happen, he would have to come up with the money to purchase Brian's interest.

When Steve and Brian became partners, they entered into a buy-sell agreement that required Steve to pay Brian's estate $360,000.

They had been in the process of purchasing life insurance policies to fund the buy-sell obligations. Unfortunately, Brian died before the funding was completed. It was like a bad dream for Steve. Or, as he says, "déjà vu all over again!" When Howard pulled the trigger on the Russian Roulette clause in their buy-sell agreement, Steve had to find $325,000 to buy him out. That led him to Harvey Feldman and eventually Brian Kvasnick. Now he was right back in the same situation. And just as in 1987, Steve didn't have the money. But this time he didn't want to look for another partner. He'd had enough partners to last him a lifetime.

"Maybe," he thought, "I can get the money by refinancing the Minnetonka store."

It was a good thought. Steve was able to find a local bank that would lend him the money he needed to purchase Brian's interest from his estate. In 1996 Steve became the sole owner of the Market and remains so to this day.

Proclamation

| WHEREAS: | Market Bar-B-Que, located at 1414 Nicollet Avenue in Minneapolis and 15320 Wayzata Boulevard in Minnetonka, was founded by the Polski family who continue to run the business today; and |

| WHEREAS: | Known locally and nationally for the quality of its food, Market Bar-B-Que has had testimonials from *Newsweek* magazine and Jay Leno, among many others; and |

| WHEREAS: | Market Bar-B-Que maintains a strong commitment to its customers, employees and the communities in which it operates, helping to make Minnesota a better place to live and work; and |

| WHEREAS: | Real pit-smoked ribs from Market Bar-B-Que have satisfied thousands of diners throughout the years; and |

| WHEREAS: | Market Bar-B-Que is celebrating fifty years of business in the State of Minnesota; |

NOW THEREFORE, I, ARNE H. CARLSON, Governor of the State of Minnesota, do hereby proclaim Tuesday, October 8, 1996 to be

MARKET BAR-B-QUE DAY

in Minnesota.

IN WITNESS WHEREOF, I have hereunto set my hand and caused the Great Seal of the State of Minnesota to be affixed at the State Capitol this eighth day of October in the year of our Lord one thousand nine hundred and ninety-six, and of the State the one hundred thirty-eighth.

_____
GOVERNOR

In 1996 Governor Arne Carlson issued a proclamation proclaiming October 8 as Market Bar-B-Que day, in honor of its fiftieth anniversary in business.

17 No Rest for the Weary

Despite the challenges Steve now faced, business continued to be good. But beginning in 1991, it became more difficult for customers, especially new ones, to navigate their way in to the Minnetonka Market, due to the fact that Wayzata Boulevard had become part of Interstate 394, and the stoplight at the intersection of Wayzata Boulevard and the frontage road providing access to the restaurant had been removed. While the problem was alleviated somewhat by the construction of a new service road leading to the restaurant, a few years later that road was torn up. Finding the Minnetonka Market was now like looking for a needle in a haystack. Though the restaurant continued to be profitable, the decline in revenue was dramatic.

The business in Minnetonka continued to keep its head above water until the evening of December 5, 2010. Steve was on duty at Minnetonka that night. He closed the restaurant at midnight and headed home through the frigid darkness—no more than a five-minute drive. He got home, took off his coat, and started to unwind from a long day at work when the phone rang. It was a little late for him to be receiving a call, but not totally unusual. Steve picked up the phone.

"Hello."

"Mr. Polski?"

"Yes, this is Mr. Polski. Who are you?"

"I'm with the Minnetonka Police Department, and I'm calling to let you know there's water gushing out of the door of your restaurant."

"How do you know that?"

"A customer drove by and called us."

"OK. Thanks for letting me know. I'll drive out there and take a look."

Steve was more aggravated about having to go back out into the cold winter evening than worried about the restaurant. He'd had two recent water problems, both involving pinhole leaks in a copper pipe caused by the buildup of minerals in the water. Maybe, he thought, a sprinkler head broke again. But when he reached the restaurant he realized this was a much bigger problem. Water was pouring out of the bricks and the front door. He opened the outside wooden door and was greeted by a wave of water. He looked through the glass vestibule and saw pieces of furniture bobbing around like corks in four feet of water. He called the water department, and a workman came out immediately but couldn't find the shut-off valve. Because the building was constructed before the city kept any records of building water systems, the worker had no idea where to look. Steve returned to his car, started the engine to keep warm, and waited in the parking lot until the next morning. About 8:00 a.m. a supervisor from the water department arrived, and turned off the water in the whole neighborhood. But it was way too late for Steve and the Minnetonka Market; tens of thousands of gallons of water had poured through the restaurant. As the water subsided, Steve was finally able to enter the restaurant, where he found four-foot watermarks on the walls and kitchen equipment still bobbing around. The place was a disaster.

Later that morning Steve received a phone call from a woman in the Minnetonka Health Department.

"I understand you've had some water out there. Are you planning on opening tonight?"

"Why don't you come over and check it out," Steve sarcastically suggested.

The woman came out and was shocked by what she saw.

"Oh my God! This is much worse than I thought."

"Yeh. We're not opening tonight."

Eventually, workers discovered what had happened. A ten-inch water main under the building had been held in place by metal straps. After thirty-five years of moisture, the straps had rusted out and given way. When that happened, the pipe shifted, and nothing could've prevented the water from flowing into the restaurant.

The damage was so extensive that there was no simple repair solution. Steve's only reasonable option would have been to raze the building and rebuild it, but the cost of doing that was prohibitive. His only remaining choice was to give up the ghost—abandon the Minnetonka location and collect the insurance proceeds. Unfortunately, as a result of the recession, by 2010 the fair market value of the building had shrunk to half the price Steve and Howard paid for it twenty-five years earlier. Steve collected the insurance money and closed the restaurant.

Today a Youngstead Tire Company outlet sits on the Minnetonka Market's former location.

A few of the booths in the dining room at the current Market Barbeque at 1414 Nicollet Avenue South

18 Famous Customers

Anyone entering the Market Barbeque for the first time is immediately welcomed by walls of photographs featuring the celebrities who have dined there since it opened in 1946. Many of them became regular customers. The Twin Cities have always attracted top name performing artists. With venues like the Orpheum Theater, the Flame Room in the Radisson Hotel, Freddie's, the Nicollet Hotel, the Prom Ballroom, and Northrup Auditorium on the campus of the University of Minnesota, to name just a few, there were plenty of places to perform. Whether they were musicians, comedians, dancers—you name it—many of them showed up at the Market late at night to eat after their gigs had ended, and the joint was jumping. Sports figures also stopped by regularly. Many loved to come to the

Market after a game or a fight, or, in some cases, if they just happened to be in town.

One evening, "Smokin'" Joe Frazier, then the world heavyweight champion, came into the Glenwood Market with his trainer for some ribs. They sat in the rear of the dining room. Smokin' Joe was quite gracious. He signed autographs and took a picture with Steve. Sadly, the picture was lost when the Market moved from Glenwood to Nicollet.

A number of years later another world heavyweight champion showed up at the Nicollet Market. Steve's son Anthony was on duty when the phone rang.

"Somebody famous is coming to eat," said the voice at the other end of the line.

"Great. We'll set you up in one of our private dining rooms. How soon shall we expect you? Oh, and how many people should we expect?"

"Soon," was the response.

Anthony had no idea who was coming, but he made sure the private dining room was set up. Fifteen minutes later three large men appeared and told Anthony that the famous person about to arrive was Mike Tyson. Tyson wanted chicken, but Anthony was told not to serve him any onions. Onions couldn't be present anywhere in the room where they were eating. Anthony assured the men there would be no onions.

Tyson and his entourage arrived a few minutes later and looked over the restaurant and the private dining room where they were to be served.

"No, no go," is all Tyson said. And with that, he and his entourage exited the restaurant, taking the chicken dinners with them.

"He must have smelled the onions," was Anthony's reaction.

Sugar Ray Leonard, another great boxing champion, also enjoyed the Glenwood Market ribs. He never came into the restaurant without his bodyguards.

Minneapolis Lakers' basketball great George Mikan and friends

George Mikan, the legendary star of the old Minneapolis Lakers basketball team, was another regular. Standing 6'10", with bad knees from traversing the basketball court, Mikan could sit only at a table where he had room to extend his long legs. The Market accommodated him by setting aside a special table that was always available for him.

Willard's, and later Steve's, great love of baseball was rewarded by visits from many great ballplayers. One evening Boog Powell, first baseman for the Baltimore Orioles, came in. He sat down in a booth and ordered a glass of milk. Steve noticed this and thought, *What a great athlete Powell is, drinking milk.* About a half an hour later, Powell staggered out of the restaurant, a bottle of scotch held close to his chest. Steve thought to himself, *I guess Boog Powell's cocktail of choice is scotch and milk.*

On another late evening or, more accurately, one early morning after the Baltimore Orioles had completed a baseball game with the Minnesota Twins, Baltimore pitchers Jim Palmer, Ross Grimsley, and Mike Torrez stopped by. Each was outfitted in an expensive suit. All

Moose Skowrin (left) and friend

three were tall and very good looking. Steve recognized Jim Palmer and introduced himself. Palmer then introduced Steve to Grimsley and Torrez. Mike Torrez became a good customer, returning to the Market frequently.

One of Steve's favorite stories is about an evening in 1977 when he got a phone call from another well-known baseball player who came into the Market whenever his team was in town for a series with the Twins.

"Steve, let's you and I go out tonight and hit some bars."

"Sounds good, Joe.[1] I'll meet you at the restaurant," was Steve's quick response. *What can be better than spending an evening with this guy,* he thought to himself.

They met up after the game and began an evening of barhopping. Eventually, they landed at the Loon Bar[2] on the corner of Fifth Street

---

[1] Not the man's real name.
[2] Now the Loon Cafe.

and First Avenue North, just a few blocks from the Glenwood Market. Joe was six feet five inches tall, with sallow skin, and he was wearing a navy blue Armani suit tailor-made for his tall, muscular body; wherever they went, he towered over the other patrons and definitely stood out in the crowd. Passing women eyeballed him. Finally, at the Loon, two beautiful blonds strike his fancy, and he starts talking to them. Joe then turns to Steve.

"So Steve, where's the snow?"

"Joe, it's August. We don't have snow here until December."

"No, Steve, you don't get it. *Snow,*" and points to his nose.

"Oh, that kind of snow!"

Steve doesn't use cocaine, but he knows where he can get some.

"Ok, Joe. I'll get you what you want. Meet me back at the Market in twenty minutes."

"OK, you go get it, and I'll pay you for it."

Steve leaves Joe and the two blonds to go to another bar where he's pretty sure he can buy some "snow" there from the manager. Steve finds him sitting at the bar.

"Hi Freddy,[3] how ya doing?"

"I'm good, Steve. What brings you to my place?"

"I'm trying to do a favor for a friend and thought you might be able to help me out. I need an ounce of cocaine."

Freddy's jaw starts swirling. He looks nervously at Steve.

"Steve, I don't want to talk about this in public. C'mon into my office."

Steve follows Freddy to the rear of the bar and his office. They walk in and Freddy locks the door behind them.

"Steve, you want to buy an OUNCE of cocaine?"

"Yeh. It's $125, right?"

"Steve, don't you mean a gram? An ounce is a huge amount. There's over twenty-eight grams in an ounce."

---

[3] Not the man's real name.

"Whoops. Right. I meant a gram."

'OK, Steve, give me a few minutes."

Freddy returned a few minutes later and handed Steve a small vial of cocaine. Steve gave him the $125 and walked over to the Market, where Joe and the two blonds were waiting for him. Steve handed the vial of cocaine to Joe, who disappeared into the rear dining room with the women.

The next day, against the Twins, Joe was the starting pitcher. He was blown out in the first inning.

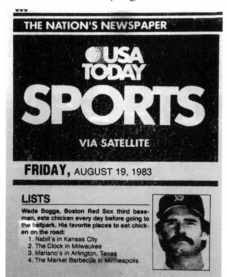

Another ballplayer who became a regular customer at the Market was Wade Boggs, the slugging third baseman for the Boston Red Sox. Boggs, like many baseball players, was superstitious. He always ate chicken before a game. Once, when being interviewed by local sportscaster Mark Rosen, Boggs mentioned his superstition.

"When I'm in Minneapolis," he said, "I eat fried chicken at the Market Barbecue."

Sometimes Boggs came in with teammates Dwight Evans and Carl Yastrzemski, who also became regulars whenever the Red Sox were in town. One evening, the two stopped by with sportswriter Sid Hartman. Steve and Evans already knew each other, but Steve had never met Yastrzemski, so he introduced himself. Yaz asked Steve if he had any broads available.

"Well, I'm a purveyor of meat, but not necessarily of that kind. If anything turns up, I'll send them your way."

Steve (center) with Carl Yastrzemski (left) and Dwight Evans

Steve left the ballplayers eating their ribs and returned to the front of the restaurant. A little later, two dancers from Goofy's Bar came in for a bite to eat. Steve approached them.

"You know who I am," he said. "I'm not trying to pimp you or anything like that, but there are two Boston Red Sox baseball players sitting in the booth over there. One of them is young and handsome and the other one is a cinch to become a Hall-of-Famer. If you're interested, after you finish dinner, go over to their table and introduce yourselves. You're on your own."

The dancers finished their meal and wandered over to the booth where Yastrzemski and Evans were seated.

"Which of you guys has red socks on?"

Yastrzemski was chewing on a rib when he heard the girl's question. The rib dropped out of his mouth. Steve has no idea what happened next.

One evening Perry Como came into the Glenwood Market for some ribs. He sat down in a booth with Willard. Several other customers spotted Como and approached his booth looking for an autograph.

"Please don't bother Mr. Como. He's eating," Willard said.

"No, no, Willard. It's okay. These are the people who made me, and I'm happy to give them an autograph."

One weekday afternoon, Gelsey Kirkland and Richard Schafer were having lunch at the Market. They were the only people in the restaurant at the time except for Steve, and they were seated in a booth near the cash register. Steve had no idea who they were but was pretty certain they had something to do with ballet. Both were tall, very thin, and very good looking. They *looked* like dancers. Steve went over to their booth and introduced himself.

"Where you from?" he asked.

"I'm from Texas," Richard replied.

"Is she your girlfriend?"

"Yeh, why do you ask?"

"I thought most ballet people were gay."

"No, no. I like girls, and I like Gelsey."

Richard Schafer is a ballet master who taught ballet at the American Ballet Theatre. Gelsey Kirkland is a famous ballerina who has danced with the American Ballet Theatre, the Stuttgart Ballet, and the Joffrey Ballet Company in Chicago. When Mikhail Baryshnikov took over the ABT as director in 1980, he said he would return to the ABT only if Gelsey Kirkland returned too, which she did.

Steve became good friends with both Gelsey and Richard, and Gelsey invited Steve to watch her dance the leading role in the ABT's performance of *Giselle*. Whenever the ABT performs in Minneapolis, Kelsey brings many of the dancers with her to the Market after a performance, and they eat and drink and smoke as if there's no tomorrow. One night Alexander Godunov, the famous Russian dancer who also performs with the ABT, came into the Market for a late dinner. He promised Steve that the next time he came, he'd bring along his good friend Mikhail Baryshnikov. Godunov is a man of his word. One night, according to Steve, a man came into the Market with two

Mikhail Baryshnikov

beautiful ballerinas, one on each arm. The little bitty man was none other than Mikhail Baryshnikov. (Baryshnikov, at 5'6", looked small beside Godunov, who is 6'3".)

"I veel eat back zer," Baryshnikov informed Steve in a thick Russian accent, pointing to the rear dining room at the Glenwood Market.

"I don't have a server back there."

"You veel be ze server."

"OK," was Steve's quick response.

Steve assumed his waiter personality. All three of them ordered the same thing—chicken and ribs—and they ate like horses.

"Mmm, mmm. Very good," said Baryshnikov.

Baryshnikov came back again the next night, but this time he was alone. He had three words of instruction for Steve: "Een ze back."

Another customer is Debbie Kepley. A former cheerleader for the Dallas Cowboys, Kepley also appeared in a *Playboy Magazine* photo spread on NFL cheerleaders, and she was in Minneapolis performing in a road show production of *Old Calcutta* at the Orpheum Theater. She came into the Market one night after a performance and approached Steve.

"Are you the proprietor, sir?"

"Yes I am, ma'am. What can I do for you?"

"Well, I just finished a performance of *Old Calcutta* at the Orpheum, and I'm starving. Will you come sit with me while I eat? I don't want to sit alone."

Steve didn't hesitate. He led Debbie to a quiet table and sat down with her. She told him about the play and a little bit about her background. And she continued to come in every night after the show to eat. On one of those late evenings, she approached Steve again.

"Are you going to be here Saturday night around midnight?"

"Yes I am."

"Well, I've got a big surprise for you."

Steve with Debbie Kepley and other members of the cast of *Oh, Calcutta.*

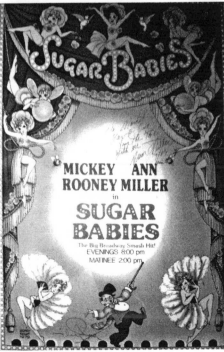

Signed posters from touring productions of Broadway shows that line the walls of the Market

Some of the Market's famous customers, from upper left: Hal Holbrook, Krusher Kowolski, Mae West (and friend), Neville Mariner, Liberace, and Nat King Cole

Steve was excited and wondered what the surprise might be. That Saturday night, at midnight, Debbie arrived at the Market, but this time she wasn't alone. She was accompanied by several people. She went up to Steve, puts her arms around him, and proceeded to give him a kiss as one of the men with her looked on, smiling.

"Steve, this is my husband. I've told him all about you!"

Debbie Kepley, like so many of the celebrities that returned repeatedly to the Market, did so not only because she liked the food, but also because of the personal attention she received from Steve whenever she visited the restaurant. In return, she gave Steve two tickets to a performance of *Old Calcutta*. The seats were great, front and center, and during the opening monologue one of the performers mentioned the Market Barbecue as a great place for ribs.

The singer Lena Horne came to Minneapolis in the 1980s to perform at the Orpheum Theater. She ate the ribs from the Glenwood Market, but never in the restaurant. Lena couldn't tolerate air conditioning, couldn't eat in a restaurant that used it, and wouldn't perform in a theater running its air-conditioning system. The Orpheum turned off its system during her performances. She rode from the Orpheum to the Market in a limousine and waited in the car while Steve delivered ribs to her.

In 1992, *Sugar Babies* was performed at the Orpheum Theater, just a few blocks from the Nicollet Market. The play featured Carol Channing but also included Mickey Rooney. Mickey came into the restaurant late one evening after a performance. Steve immediately recognized him, of course, welcomed him to the Market, and introduced himself. Mickey was gracious and invited Steve to sit with him while he was eating. Mickey was apparently starving; he devoured his ribs voraciously. Due to his significant paunch, substantial evidence of his meal began to appear on his shirt.

Steve learned that Mickey had a type of germ phobia that made him reluctant to shake hands with people. When several customers came over to the table requesting autographs, instead of shaking their hands he rubbed elbows with them. And every once in a while he forgot the phobia and shook the person's hand impulsively. Steve found Mickey Rooney to be very pleasant and responsive, but when he asked him about his old movies or his relationship with Judy Garland, Mickey preferred not to respond. "I don't live in the past," he told Steve.

Virtually all of the sports figures and celebrities that have visited the Market over the years have made a positive impression on Steve—but there are exceptions. One night, around 2:00 a.m., Red Skelton came into the Glenwood Market for some ribs. Steve was delighted—he had always been a big fan. He especially liked the way Red closed his performances by saying, "Good night and God bless." Anyone who says that, Steve thinks, has to be a good human being. So Steve was both disillusioned and disappointed when he noticed that Mr. Skelton was not alone. With him were two "showgirls," one on each arm.

Many members of the Twin Cities media have also been frequent customers at both the Glenwood and Nicollet Markets. Dave Moore, the popular newscaster for WCCO-TV, often celebrated his birthday at the restaurant. According to Steve, his uncle Perry introduced Dave to his wife. Steve also remembers Dave as helping him with his thesis when he was in college.

Dave often came in following the 10 p.m. newscast, and he always sat on a stool at the counter. If there were other famous folks in the restaurant, politicians or celebrities, Steve would invite Dave to join them. Dave's reply was always the same.

"I like to sit with the working people."

Steve Cannon, the WCCO radio personality, was another regular customer. He did a number of radio commercials for the restaurant and frequently plugged it on his show. He often showed up for a meal with his wife, son, or both.

A few of the sports stars who stopped by the Market, clockwise from upper left: Harmon Killebrew, Sugar Ray Leonard and friend, Whitey Ford, Jim Fregosi, Roger Maris, Jesse Ventura, Willie Mays, and (center) Bud Grant

The great blues singer B.B. King came to Minneapolis in 2012 for a performance at the State Theater. Following his performance, he was hungry, and his agent called the Nicollet Market. Steve Pust, the bartender, answered the phone. "Hello. Market Barbecue. How can I help you?"

"I'm calling for B.B. King. Mr. King wants to order a pulled chicken sandwich to go."

"No problem. I'll have it ready for you in ten minutes," Steve Pust responded, quite excited that B.B. King was coming to the Market.

Steve Polski, who was standing nearby, was also delighted that B.B. King was coming. There was one small problem in filling the order. A pulled chicken sandwich isn't on the Market's menu. Pulled pork, but no pulled chicken. Nonetheless, Steve was determined to fill the order. He walked back to the kitchen and explained the problem to the chef, Bill Mulenburg. Bill went to work and created a pulled chicken sandwich. Steve wrapped it carefully, included some coleslaw and fries, and packaged the order for take-out. A few minutes later, someone appeared and picked up the order.

A half hour later, the phone rang again. This time Steve answered.

"Market Barbecue. This is Steve. How can I help you?"

"I'm the guy who picked up the sandwich for B.B. King. He asked me to call you to let you know B.B. says that was the best pulled chicken sandwich he's ever had. Now he wants to order two chicken dinners."

Of all the famous people who have become Market customers, Jay Leno is one of the most loyal and regular supporters. His love affair with the Market began at the Glenwood location long before he became associated with the *Tonight Show*. One weekday afternoon, Steve was standing outside of the restaurant around 3:30. The restaurant's normal hours of operation were from 11:00 to 2:30, reopening at 5:00 p.m. for dinner. The afternoon break gave Steve time to do his bookkeeping when there wouldn't have been much business anyway. As Steve relaxed outside, a Dodge Omni drove up and two men got out. One of them was a man of considerable bulk. They started walking toward the entrance to the restaurant.

"Excuse me, guys," Steve said. "Are you coming to the Market?"

"Yeh."

The restaurant may have been "officially" closed, but Steve's policy is never to turn away a customer, no matter what time it is.

"Well, we're closed until five, but if you don't mind me cooking for you, c'mon in," Steve told them.

The men entered the restaurant, sat down in a booth, and both ordered a full slab of ribs. After taking their order, Steve went back to the kitchen, put the order together—it took only about ten minutes—and returned to the table with the food. He then walked away to let the two customers eat in peace.

"Hey, where are you going? Why don't you sit down with us?" the smaller of the two men said to Steve.

Steve was happy to oblige. He sat down with them, and they started talking. The big guy introduced himself as Scott Hanson, a local comedian. The other guy's name was Jay Leno. Steve has never heard of either of them. Hanson told Steve that Leno was also a comedian and was in town to do a gig with Hanson at the Comedy Club.

They both loved the ribs and the restaurant. And that was the beginning of a long love affair between Jay Leno, Scott Hanson, and the Market that continues to this day. Every time Jay comes to Minneapolis, he stops at the Market. Many times Jay calls Steve to let him know he's in town.

"Hi Steve. I'm in town and I'll be there tonight around 9 o'clock."

Sure enough, come 9 o'clock, Jay walks into the Market.

Jay never comes with an entourage. He's usually dressed in blue jeans and is driving a modest car. Steve always sets up a table for him in one of the Market's private dining rooms, to give him some privacy, but Jay often prefers to mingle with the other customers.

Steve (left) with Jay Leno (center) and Scott Hanson

"Steve, would it be all right for me to go talk to some of your customers?"

"Of course, Jay. Feel free to do whatever you want."

So Jay leaves his table in the private dining room, enters the main dining room, and approaches people at their tables. The customers tend to be surprised and couldn't be more delighted.

As Jay became more popular, he got increasing attention from the Twin Cities media. On one occasion in 1989 he was interviewed at the airport by a reporter from Channel 4.

"Jay, what are you doing in town?"

"I'm flying back to New York, but I had to stop in Minneapolis so I could go to the Market Barbecue."

"No, really Jay. What are you doing here?"

"I told you. I'm here to go to the Market Barbecue."

"Jay, really?"

"I don't know what else to tell you. I'll be at the Market Barbecue at 11 o'clock."

And he was there at 11. He was doing a benefit performance and it wasn't supposed to be publicized, so he used the Market as his cover.

On another evening Jay came into the restaurant ,and Steve approached him with a request.

"You know, Jay, we've been friends a long time. Can I ask a favor of you?"

"Sure."

"My son, Anthony, is thirteen, and he's a big fan. He asked me if I could get your autograph for him."

"No problem."

Jay grabbed a napkin, drew a caricature of his face with an elongated jaw—his motif—and signed it. Then he said to Steve, "You know, we can do better than that. Call him up."

So Steve called home. When Anthony answered, he handed the phone to Jay.

"Hello."

"Hey, kid, it's Jay Leno."

"Really?"

"Yeh. How ya doing? What grade are you in?"

The next day at school, Anthony couldn't wait to tell his friends about the call.

"Hey, guess who called me last night? Jay Leno."

"Oh yeh. Sure. Mickey Mantle called me."

"John Wayne called me."

No one believed him. Anthony told Steve what happened, and Steve was determined to help Anthony prove to his friends that Jay Leno really had called him. So Steve called Cheryl Johnson, the columnist for the *Minneapolis Star Tribune* better known as C.J., to tell her the story. C.J. liked the story and included it in her column the next day. Anthony took a copy of the article to his friends. No one doubts him now.

Leno has plugged the Market more than once on the *Tonight Show*, and Steve has sent ribs to Leno via Federal Express. In 2013, Jay came to town to headline the annual Neighborhood Health Care Pace Center Gala at the Minneapolis Convention Center. Following his performance, Leno dined on a slab of ribs from the Market delivered to him in his dressing room by C.J. and Anthony Polski.

FACES & PLACES

C.J.

Leno & friends get a ribbing

Market BBQ's Steve Polski delivers for longtime pal

If Market BBQ pigs could fly, **Jay Leno** wouldn't have needed delivery from **Steve Polski**. The "Tonight Show" host jetted into the Twin Cities Tuesday for an appearance at the Minneapolis Convention Center before what's described as the Super Bowl of convention planners. Before flying in for a gig that I'm guessing paid close to $200,000, Leno ordered up his No. 2 priority: ribs to go from his longtime buddy at Market BBQ. Polski has known Jay since way before anybody was paying him six figures for a couple of hours of work. He loaded the ribs and fixin's into the waiting Escalade while Leno was still on stage killin'. Although Leno looked absolutely whupped — even the bags under his eyes appeared tired — he still had a couple of jokes left for the ribs man and his entourage: **Anthony Polski,** Steve's son; **Kris Humphries,** Polski family friend and NBA rookie of the year hopeful; and **Michael Rainville,** an official at

Jay Leno's backstage appearance at the Minneapolis Convention Center was over quickly for Anthony Polski, left, his father, Market BBQ's Steve Polski, and NBA rookie of the year hopeful Kris Humphries, right. Leno was in town to speak at the American Society of Association Executives convention.

"After I have my rookie of the year season, he has to have me on his show." Leno left before I could say there's something

tidbit we really care about in the Twin Cities is this: "I know [Kevin Garnett] got married." It reportedly happened at his

Preparing take-out orders prior to the lunch-hour rush

19 The Employees

The employees at Market Barbecue have found it to be a good place to work. Turnover has been modest, and several employees have been on the staff for decades.

Charlotte Wheeler started working for Willard and Sam as a waitress at the Glenwood Market shortly after it opened its doors in 1962. When the restaurant moved from Glenwood to Nicollet, Charlotte went with it and became a cashier/hostess until she retired in 2004.

Becky Zepeda worked with Charlotte at the Nicollet Market and remembers her well. She describes Charlotte as "a gravel-voiced old lady surrounded by a cloud of cigarette smoke." Charlotte may have been old, but, according to Becky, she was strong and she was tough. One evening when Becky was waitressing, she heard a commotion coming from the front desk. Looking over, she saw Charlotte "yelling her head off" as she struggled to stop a guy who was trying to get his hands into the cash register. Charlotte pushed back, shoving the man into the menu stand near the front desk, which caused it to come off its hinges. She then chased the man down the back hallway and out the back door into the parking lot, swearing all the way.

Becky started working at the Nicollet Market in 1992, when she was nineteen years old. In her own words, she "has loved the place and the job since the beginning." She has her own memories of celebrities coming to dine at the Nicollet Market. One evening when she was working, Johnny Mathis, the great vocalist, came in for dinner along with an entourage of twelve guests. Becky remembers Johnny as being very gracious and readily signing autographs for the waitresses.

On another occasion, when Charlotte Wheeler was in charge of the front desk and the cash register, a tall, handsome man came into the Market to place an order to take out some fried chicken. Charlotte had no idea who he was (and wouldn't have cared even if she knew, since she treated all customers exactly the same), but Becky and the other waitresses immediately recognized the man as the actor Keanu Reeves. They were all excited as they watched Reeves sitting on the bench next to the front desk, waiting patiently for his order. After sitting there for a few minutes, he stood up and approached Charlotte.

"Excuse me, but could I please have some baked beans with my order?"

"OK, but that's going to be another $1.50."

"That will be fine," Reeves replied, smiling.

Mike Hamond began working at the Glenwood Market in 1978 when he was twenty-one. He got the job through his uncle, who was a boxer and a friend of Sam and Willard. Mike started his career at the Market as a part-time line cook. Today he's a full-time cook, spending all of his time in the Market's kitchen. Mike also worked Saturdays at the Minnetonka Market before it closed in 2010. Since he works in the kitchen, Mike doesn't have much of an opportunity to see or meet any of the restaurant's famous customers, but he does remember shaking hands with Carl Eller, the great Minnesota Viking defensive end.

Long-time cook Mike Hamond

Scott Horowitz began working at the Minnetonka Market in 1985, just a month or two after the restaurant opened. He served as a manager at both the Minnetonka and Nicollet locations until he left in 2003. Scott remembers the first day he was in charge of the Minnetonka Market. He was working at the cash register when he

Missy Nelson, one of the veteran line cooks, gathers wood for the fire at the woodpile behind the restaurant. She was raised in a house heated with wood.

heard the back door open, then heard footsteps in the kitchen. Suddenly two very dapper men appeared wearing suits, wide neckties, and fedoras with a feather inserted in the band. To Scott they looked like characters out of *The Godfather.* Having no idea who they were and fearing there was about to be some trouble, Scott went into the office, locked the door, and called Steve, who was at the Glenwood Market.

"Steve, I don't know how to explain this, but I think that the Mafia is here."

"Calm down, Scott," Steve responded. "Describe the men to me."

"Well, one of them is wearing a fedora with a felt band and a feather in it."

"That's Sam," Steve chuckled.

"The other guy is wearing a long, blue, felt coat that covers him from his neck to his feet. It's open at the chest, and I can see his broad, brown polka dot tie," Scott continued.

"Willard," Steve responded, still laughing. "Sam's my uncle and

Willard's my dad. Don't worry, Scott. You're not being set up. Go back into the restaurant and introduce yourself."

A few weeks later Steve instructed Scott to drive downtown to the Glenwood Market to pick up some supplies for Minnetonka. Scott parked his car near the rear door, making sure he took the car keys with him, and went into the Glenwood Market to pick up the supplies. Willard handed him the package, and Scott headed back out the rear door to his car. The transaction took no more than two or three minutes, but Scott's car was missing. Scott ran back into the restaurant.

"Willard, my car is gone. It's been stolen," Scott cried.

Willard looked at him and started laughing in the same way Steve did when Scott thought the Mafia was paying him a visit.

"Scottie, my boy. Don't worry. I'll get your car back for you," Willard said.

Willard then made a very short phone call. Scott had no idea whom he called or what he said, but two minutes later, his car was back, unharmed, exactly where he had parked it.

Willard instructed the driver to come into the restaurant.

"See that young man over there?" he said, pointing at Scott. "That's Scottie, and he belongs to me."

From that moment on, Scott was "Scottie," and his car was never touched again.

One evening when Scott was on duty as the manager at the Nicollet Market, Steve Cannon came in.

"Scottie, have you seen Morgan Mundane? He's supposed to meet me here for a very important meeting. Please send him over to my table as soon as you spot him."

Morgan Mundane was one of the self-voiced characters Cannon created on his radio show and whom he collectively called the "L'il Cannons." Others included Ma Linger and Back Lash Larue.

Nancy Ryan worked as a waitress at the Minnetonka Market until she and her husband, Tom, moved to Hartsville, Tennessee. In 2010, Tom's son, Myron Roggeman, who lived in Elk River, Minnesota, called the Nicollet Market. Steve was on duty and answered the call.

"Mr. Polski, this is Myron Roggeman. My dad is Tom Ryan, and two weeks ago he was diagnosed with terminal cancer. He's already lost twelve pounds. He told his doctor, 'You've got to get me better long enough to eat some ribs from the Market Barbecue in Minneapolis before I croak.'"

The next day, Steve shipped $300 worth of ribs to Tom Ryan in Hartsville.

Beginning in 1972, the employees at the Glenwood Market affiliated with the Hotel Employees and Restaurant Employees Local 17. The affiliation worked well for both the employees and management until 9/11. Following the national tragedy, many conventions in the city were canceled. This in turn caused a substantial decline in business at the restaurant. In this economic climate, the amount the Market was paying to the Union became prohibitive, and in 2007 the Market's employees voted unanimously to disaffiliate from the union. Today the Market continues to have no relationship with the union.

20 Today, Anthony, and the Future

Many things have affected the Market since it opened its doors in 1946. Many of the customers who frequented the North Seventh Street and later the Glenwood locations were from the Greatest Generation—a term coined by journalist Tom Brokaw to describe the generation that grew up in the United States during the Great Depression and either fought in World War II or otherwise contributed to the war effort. Once the war was over, many of these young Americans wanted only one thing—to have fun. They liked to drink, eat, and stay up late. The Market was the perfect place for them. As this generation grew older and eventually passed away, there was no group to replace them, no new generation with a similar zest for going out and socializing as they did. Part of the reason for this may be the prosperity that followed the war and the resulting work ethic. Most people seemed to be more concerned with making a living and raising a family than with playing, especially late-night playing. The Market's peak business used to begin after 11 p.m., when the bars started closing and people were looking for a place to eat. Today most of the business is at lunch and dinner time, not late at night. That means less drinking. Today, about 75 percent of the Market's revenue is from food sales, and only 25 percent from the sale of alcohol.

Another change from the "old days" is that celebrities don't show up at the restaurant as often as they used to. The entertainment business has changed. Today, most gigs are single evening performances

instead of week-long engagements. Often a celebrity will fly in and out of town on the same day. But that doesn't mean the Market's food doesn't continue to attract celebrities. It does. Instead of eating at the restaurant, many of them send someone from their entourage to pick up their order so that they can enjoy their late-night meal in the privacy of their dressing room or hotel room. Often the order is packed so performers can take the food with them on the plane and enjoy it at home.

Steve's decision in 1987 to move the restaurant from Glenwood Avenue to its current location on Nicollet, to take advantage of business from the city's new convention center, has paid off in spades. Business almost always spikes when there's a major convention in the city.

In 2009 a mathematicians' convention was in town. One morning around 10:45, a gentleman entered the Market looking for an early lunch.

"Are you open?" he asked Steve.

"We don't open for another fifteen minutes, but I'd be happy to take care of you."

The customer introduced himself to Steve.

"My name is Gregory Tang. I'm a mathematician, and I'm in town for the math convention at the Convention Center. Let me take a look at your menu. I'd also be interested in any recommendations you might have."

"Our signature item is spare ribs," Steve tells him.

"That's not going to work so well for where I'm going. What sandwich would you suggest?"

"The barbecue beef brisket is excellent."

"Sounds good. I'll take one for now and one for later."

Mr. Tang finishes his sandwich quickly. He takes the other sandwich and heads back to the Convention Center. About 6 o'clock that evening a stream of customers, all from the math convention, come into the restaurant for dinner. Steve asks them how they heard about the Market. They tell him Gregory Tang was the principal speaker at the convention and addressed the group at noon. At the end of his presentation, he asked everyone in the audience to take out a pencil and paper.

"If there is anything you must do while in Minneapolis, it's go to the Market Barbecue."

Steve's curiosity is piqued. Who is Gregory Tang? Later that evening Steve does a little research on the Internet and discovers that Tang is quite famous. He's written several bestselling books, including the *Grapes of Math*. Steve sends Tang an email message thanking him for the referrals. Tang responds by asking how well the spare ribs travel. Will they survive Federal Express? Steve assures him they will do just fine. Mr. Tang then places an order and Steve happily sends it to him via FedEx.

Steve Polski continues to be the sole owner of the Market, and you can almost always find him at the Market any weekday between noon and three o'clock, but just like his own father did, Steve has turned over the day-to-day operations to his son Anthony. Anthony,

Anthony and Steve inspect some chicken in the wood-fired oven.

like his father, began working at the Market as a dishwasher. That job was at the Minnetonka Market when he was thirteen. Continuing to travel the same path as Steve, Anthony next learned how to cook, and before he graduated from high school, he'd learned how to tend bar. Following his graduation from the University of Minnesota in 2003 and a four-year absence from the family business, Anthony returned to the Nicollet Market, where he learned how to run the front of the house, how to cashier, and how to be a good maître d'.

While respecting the history of the Market and the traditions he's inherited from his father and grandfather are very important to Anthony, his focus is on making certain the restaurant continues to thrive in a rapidly changing restaurant environment.

"I love our ribs and chicken and all the food on our menu. I believe in the method we use for cooking our chicken and ribs. I don't want to change any of that. But I also want to make sure we do whatever we need to do to ensure that our food is available in whatever form our customers choose—eating at the restaurant, picking up food to eat at home, or having us deliver our ribs to their door. I also want to make sure that we attract out-of-town visitors to the Market, especially those folks in town for a convention or a ball game."

Anthony has a strong work ethic. He works seven days a week and does anything and everything needed to maintain the restaurant, including cleaning up after the last customer has left.

"Why pay someone to do something if you can do it yourself?" says Anthony.

Anthony believes there is a great opportunity to grow by increasing the Market's catering and take-out businesses. Among its major catering customers are the Minnesota Twins and the clubhouse of the visiting team. Anthony also is focused on increasing the Market's take-out business. He is doing this by referrals and word-of-mouth advertising.

I asked Steve what Anthony's official position or title is at the Market.

"Anthony's official title is 'Next in Line.'"

C.J., the columnist and good friend of Steve and of the Market, often refers to Anthony in her column as "owner-in-waiting."

Epilogue

The Market Barbecue today bears little resemblance to the original establishment founded sixty-nine years ago at 130 North Seventh Street, or to its second location at 28 Glenwood Avenue. The North Seventh Street address no longer exists, and the Glenwood Market location now lies buried under Interstate 394 and the Target Center. So don't bother looking for them. And you won't find any card-playing, let alone gambling, at the Market's current location at 1414 Nicollet.

Max (left), Steve (center), and Anthony

No more discounts on an Armani suit, either. Things have changed. Today the Market sells only food and drink—no clothes, no jewelry. Plenty of liquor continues to be consumed at the Market, just as it was at the North Seventh Street location, but the Nicollet Market has a liquor license and everything is aboveboard. While the bill of fare has expanded to reflect changes in eating habits since 1946, ribs and chicken still dominate the menu, and they're still cooked in a pit over an open fire, following the same recipe Willard and Sam Polski developed so long ago. Long-time customers who come to the restaurant after a long absence often tell Steve that the Market is exactly the way they remember it. While you aren't as likely to run into a celebrity having a late-evening meal at the Market, you'll be reminded of all those who have eaten there over the past sixty-nine years by the photographs lining the walls.

Steve, and now Anthony, are the beneficiaries of Willard's and Sam's struggle to climb the rungs of the "crooked ladder." The brothers' determination that they and their families would have an easier and better life culminated in the opening and then the success of the Market Barbecue. Steve, who wanted this book to be written as a tribute to his father, expresses his gratefulness and love for his dad by saying, "I'm glad my dad was born before me."

And Anthony, who's now in charge of the Market, expresses his gratitude and appreciation to Steve. While he may not do things the same way his dad did, the older he gets, the more respect he has for Steve. "When I first started working here after graduating from college, I couldn't believe how dumb my dad was," Anthony says. "Now, ten years later, I can't believe how much he has learned."

Steve's son Max also worked at the Market when he was in high school. Following his graduation from the University of Minnesota/Guthrie Theater Actor Training Program with a Bachelor in Fine Arts degree, Max embarked on an acting career. He continues to eat all of his ribs at the Market, but otherwise is not involved in its business.

Appendix: The Ribs

This story would not be not complete without at least a few words about the ribs. The pork ribs served at the Market continue to be prepared from the same recipe developed at the restaurant's original location by Fisher, the Market's first cook. The cooking process hasn't changed. After soaking in the Market's special basting sauce, the ribs are placed in a large brick pit at a specific height above the firebox that enables the smoke to penetrate the meat while the heat from the hardwood renders juices back into the fire, and in turn back into the meat. During this cooking process, the smoke is swirling around in the pit and through the ribs, thereby producing the amazing flavor that can be obtained only from a wood-burning brick pit. The ribs are lean and meaty and require no sauce. However, depending on your taste, both mild and hot sauces are available to spread on the meat.

Steaks, chicken, beef brisket and pork shoulders are prepared in the same fashion. The cooking process is a delicate one, requiring constant attention. Too long in the fire produces a rubbery texture, and too little undercooks the food.

When Willard and Sam were in charge of the Market, 90 percent of the food was either pork ribs or chicken. Other items on that original menu included beef sandwiches, fried chicken, fried chicken livers, and hamburgers. When Steve took over the operation from his dad, he began to expand the menu. He added a chicken breast sandwich, promoting it with the following ad: "Our chickens

gave up their breasts for our buns." One of the most popular new items was the pulled pork sandwich. Various cuts of beef steak have been added, including a twenty-ounce rib eye. Today the menu also includes salads, beef brisket, a ground pork burger (called the "boss hog"), and rib tips.

The best place to eat the Market's wonderful fare is at the restaurant, where you can sit in a booth and dine with the many celebrities whose photos line the walls, and who, like you, have enjoyed the Market's ribs and chicken. But if you can't make it into the restaurant to dine, Anthony and Steve will be pleased to put up your order for takeout. If you're unable to pick up your order, they'll be happy to have it delivered to your door. Just call 612-872-1111 to make a reservation or to place an order. The Polskis will take care of the details.

If the ribs need to be reheated before eating, Steve has fail-safe directions. The best option is to light a gas grill, wait until the burners are hot, and then place the ribs on the grill. Turn them over after two minutes or when the ribs begin to bubble—whichever comes first— and give them another two minutes on the grill.

If you want to reheat the ribs in an oven, place the ribs under the broiler and follow the same directions. Finally, if you're forced to use a microwave (least desirable), be careful since there's a good chance that the meat will get too tough. The same instructions also work for reheating the Market's barbecued chicken.

Acknowledgments

I've spent the better part of two years researching and writing this book. There is a long list of people to whom I'm indebted for their help and support. I want to acknowledge all of them, but I know I'm going to forget somebody. I hope they'll forgive me and know that no omission has been intentional. I'm most appreciative of the help everyone provided me.

This book could never have been written without Steve Polski. Not only did Steve ask me to write this story, but he was always available to share with me the stories that are included in the book and to answer my never-ending stream of questions. Thank you, Steve, for being so patient with me, and thanks especially for providing me the opportunity to "meet" your family and to write the incredible story of their lives.

Thanks also to Anthony Polski, who, like his dad, was always available to answer my questions.

A very special thanks to Perry Polski for sharing with me his memories of his father and brothers.

Thank you Bonnie Polski for sharing with me your memories of your father, Willard.

Thank you Michael Hammer, Scott Horowitz, and Becky Zepeda, all long-time employees of the Market, for sharing some of your experiences with me.

Thank you Ted Kueller for sharing with me your memory of Willard when he worked at Minnesota Knitting Mills.

A special thanks to Sandy Swirnoff for reading my manuscript and providing me with so many helpful suggestions.

Finally, thank you Wendy Swirnoff, my favorite daughter. You have to be the best editor a writer could wish for. Without your editing and content suggestions, this book would have been a mishmash.

AUTHOR MICHAEL SWIRNOFF (seen here on the right next to Steve Polski) is a retired attorney and former business executive. He has previously written *Be Brave, Don't Cry: A Mother's Legacy*, a personal memoir about his relationship with his mother. Mike lives in Minneapolis, Minnesota, and La Jolla, California.

NOW YOU CAN AFFORD TO MAKE A PIG OF YOURSELF